Fearless consulting

Fearless consulting

Temptations, risks and limits of the profession

Erik de Haan

John Wiley & Sons, Ltd

Other Wiley Editorial Offices

Library of Congress Cataloging-in-Publication Data
Haan, Erik de.
   [Adviseren voor gevorderden. English]
   Fearless consulting : temptations, risks, and limits of the profession / Erik de Haan.
      p. cm.
   Includes bibliographical references and index.
   ISBN-13: 978-0-470-02695-3 (cloth : alk. paper)
   ISBN-10: 0-470-02695-2 (cloth : alk. paper)
 1. Business consultants. 2. Consultants. 3. Intervention (Administrative procedure)
4. Problem solving. 5. Responsibility. I. Title.
   HD69.C6H3213 2006
   001—dc22

                    2005034533

British Library Cataloguing in Publication Data

A catalogue record for this book is available from the British Library

ISBN 13 978-0-470-02695-3 (HB)
ISBN 10 0-470-02695-2 (HB)

Translated by Sue Stewart.
Illustrations by Selma van Vemde.
Typeset in 11/13pt Goudy by SNP Best-set Typesetter Ltd., Hong Kong
Printed and bound in Great Britain by TJ International Ltd, Padstow, Cornwall, UK
This book is printed on acid-free paper responsibly manufactured from sustainable forestry in which
at least two trees are planted for each one used for paper production.

. . . for, on account of our good qualities, we shall reform the character of friends, by means of our conversation. But if on account of our good qualities, how not also of our bad ones? For, just as it is suitable on account of the good cheer of the former, so too thanks to sympathy for the latter, to endure fearless speech through which we are helped. For in fact if it is possible for you, having spoken fearlessly, to stay in the same condition: if you will withhold nothing, you will save a man who is a friend . . .

Philodemos, *Fearless speech*, around 50 BC, Fr. 43

Contents

Foreword 1

This is an extraordinary book in tackling the mostly unspoken inner dialogue of what goes on in the contact between consultant and client, and in the way Erik de Haan combines contemporary personal experience with an exceptionally broad set of sources and thinking drawn from literature, philosophy and the arts over the centuries.

It focuses these strands down in a thoughtful and sensitive way to provide new insights into the "Koans", puzzles or paradoxes which one experiences as a consultant, and how to deal with them effectively.

It is an ultimate act of bravery in a world seeking certainty and the avoidance of ambiguity, for a practising consultant to share this dialogue so openly on the dilemmas arising in the practice of this profession.

That he dares to admit the existence of these dilemmas is proof of his commitment to "fearless speaking" in the pursuit of "fearless consulting". That he is confident in his intuition is the likely outcome of his deep experience as a coach and consultant, his reflective powers, and his obvious respect and appreciation of people just as they are. The outcome is a reflective and practical book for the practising consultant.

Speaking fearlessly, I would take issue on one aspect – his four forms of Argumentation, summarised as advocacy, conversation, fearless speech and flattery, lead to an acceptance of the primacy of "fearless speaking", and to the avoidance of "flattery" in all situations. This limits too much, in my opinion, the consultant's ability not to "flatter" but to empathise, create rapport, show enthusiasm, and thereby create some emotional linkage as part of a productive relationship.

Erik, as per one of his iconic forms of Argumentation, is a "free man with ambition", and prepared to say what he thinks. His ambition is to raise and clarify the role of the consultant profession based on integrity and courage. He summarises his intention here as:

> "down with flattery, long live irony, intervene fearlessly, know thyself, and let go in time!"

This approach, he believes will give both longevity to assignments and sustainability of the profession into the future, by breaking away from the reductionist consultant habits of certainty and codification of all one encounters.

Primarily addressing "Consultants", this book would be equally valuable to coaches, mentors, facilitators and line bosses engaged in "development discussions".

It is an enjoyable and stimulating read, raising self-awareness, causing reflection, and generating ideas to improve upon – if one makes the personal choice, as Erik would point out, to do so!

Ed Green
Independent Consultant and Coach, Building Collaborative Futures

Foreword 2

The whole field of organisational development and organisational behaviour came of age in the nineteen seventies, led very much by a superb series of books published by Addison Wesley. The authors such as Warner Burke, Ed Schein, Chris Argyris, Donald Schon, and Richard Beckard, became the leaders of the so called "OD movement". Then in the nineteen eighties consultancy became associated with business re-engineering, introducing technology systems and business processes and the craft of organisational development consulting was eclipsed. In recent years we are starting to see a re-emergence of the craft with a number of new master's programmes in organisational consulting and some exciting new books by practitioners writing about their craft.

Erik de Haan is one of the most exciting writers of this new wave. He is a writer who combines clear and honest accounts of his own practice, with an intellectual rigour in a wide variety of disciplines that provide depth to his reflections on his own and other's practice. Paul Ricoeur, the hermeneutic philosopher, wrote about the near impossible challenge of combining clarity and depth in one's writing, and I was delighted to find that this book successfully brings together these two qualities.

What a joy to have a book that weaves Buddhism, psychoanalysis, hermeneutics with stories from Greek history and philosophy and from some of the great literature of the world. Also a book that provides clear models of consulting practice, with examples of interventions and illustrative case studies and yet manages to avoid the trap of providing a handbook of answers.

One of my spiritual teachers taught me that "you can judge a religion by the quality of its doubt". In my work I have taken that sentiment and applied it to the work and writings of many professions, who like the religions of old, can be entranced by their own certainties, which inhibit them from learning and developing. In my recent book "The Wise Fool's Guide to Leadership" (O Books 2005) I used the ironic stories of the great wise fool Nasrudin to unsettle the certainties of organisational development consultants and provide an unlearning curriculum for leaders. Erik is also a lover of wise fools. His previous book "The Consulting Process as Drama" brought the wisdom of King Lear's fool to inspire the modern day consultant. This, his latest book, encourages the consultant to develop irony as a core part of their interventions and draws upon Apollo and Buddha as his exemplars.

The most important contribution of Erik's book is the encouragement to all consultants to be fearless – and to practice "parrhesia" or fearless speech – to speak the truth, concerning the challenges that must be faced, without fear of the consequences. In our own work we put the practice of "ruthless compassion" at the heart of consulting relationships, to relate with empathy to those within the client system, while directly confronting what is being denied or not even recognised in the individual, team, organisation or wider system.

This book mainly concentrates on consulting where the client is an individual or team, my hope is that Erik will go on to write a sequel, where the fearless consultant has to work with whole organisations and wider systems. In the world of complex public sector partnerships and private sector global corporations, the world desperately needs more fearless consultants who can engage with the difficulties and ambiguities of complex systems.

Erik's great contribution is to show ways that the consultant can develop their fearlessness without falling into the trap of becoming heroic. His last section on tragic consulting shows that fearlessness must be combined with appropriate humility. Ultimately it is the processes of life and nature that are the greatest teachers and at best we can only help them do their work.

Dr. Peter Hawkins
Chairman of Bath Consultancy Group

Preface

This book begins where the handbooks on consulting leave off. It is a book that raises more questions than it provides answers, opens up more new possibilities than it prescribes solutions. It does refer back to the better handbooks, but attempts to go further. My aim in this book is to get consultants thinking about their profession, with questions such as

- What does "consulting" really mean?
- What does it mean to be a consultant?
- What sort of dilemmas can consulting entail?
- And how can consulting degenerate into something that is no longer consulting?

In order to answer these and other questions about consulting, I draw on a number of other reflections on consulting which are sometimes overlooked by professional consultants, such as Foucault's lectures on fearless speech, Plutarch's attempt to distinguish between a friend and a flatterer, Nietzsche's understanding of the origins of tragedy, Machiavelli's advice to rulers and their advisers, and Lear's and Vellacott's books on irony. These are books which consultants seldom read but which, in my experience, might inspire them to new and powerful interventions. I attempt to put forward the lessons from these books clearly and concisely. Where possible, I translate those lessons into specific interventions and substantiate them by giving examples from my own practice or that of other consultants.

I see consulting as a *state of mind*, an *intention* in speech which, provided it is properly translated into interventions, can be very helpful for others. The coming chapters will examine various aspects of this intention. For example, I consider consulting from the following perspectives:

- Fearless speech – with an intention that distinguishes it from flattery;
- Irony – with an intention that distinguishes it from sarcasm;
- Powerlessness – with an intention that distinguishes it from impotence;
- Non-responsibility – with an intention that distinguishes it from irresponsible behaviour;
- Tragic understanding – with an intention that distinguishes it from drama.

The book will consider a number of unsavoury questions or *koans*, riddles to which I myself, in my practice, i.e. in specific situations, often fail to find an answer:

- How can one in fact distinguish a consultant from a flatterer?
- As a consultant, how does one handle ambiguous and ambivalent clients? Can one in fact consult with ambiguity?
- Is consulting free from power?
- When is it worthwhile being irresponsible as a consultant?
- How can one let go without letting the other person go?

These are the questions with which I find myself wrestling most as a consultant, and which usually leave me in a state of bewilderment. I can do no more than to keep asking them, and to provide some new perspectives on them in this book.

When I view the consulting profession from the perspective of questions such as these, I see a profession at constant risk of losing itself: by becoming absorbed into other professions, by falling prey to an inflated sense of its own importance, or by degenerating into something primitive that is no longer consulting. The "right intention" of the consultant is in fact under constant pressure. If you are successful it is hugely tempting to start to overestimate your own interventions, to make a grab for power, or to let your consulting degenerate into flattery. If you are not successful, you fail to achieve a connection with your client and what you are doing is therefore no longer consulting either. If you remain detached you are not a consultant because you are not able to make your client the centre of your interventions; however, it is also not good to be too deeply involved because you will then start taking on responsibilities which are not within the consultant's remit. By its very nature, therefore, consulting always takes place "at the cutting edge": it is an activity that has to be won and earned again at every step of the process.

This book deals with that endless journey between Scylla and Charybdis – the devouring remorse of struggling on and taking over the client's responsibilities, and the whirlpool of inflated ego and sarcasm. Consulting is that journey between temptations and risks, which looks different every time but which, time and time again, draws the sensitive consultant into considering his or her own profession anew. Mastery in consulting, the right intention, is therefore steering the middle course, just as Aristotle described it.[1]

The shortest way to summarise the intention of consulting according to this book is: "down with flattery, long live irony, intervene fearlessly, know thyself, and let go in time!" In the 10 chapters that follow I will attempt to explain and develop this unusual motto.

I am a management consultant myself and that creates a certain bias. There are bound to be dilemmas which I have encountered to a lesser extent than, for example, lawyers, architects, doctors or policy advisers. But, on the basis of ample experience of collaborating with consultants of many types and of training others in consulting skills and style, I have confidence that many of the themes in this book will be relevant and familiar to other facilitators, advisers, experts and professionals, working both internally and externally, across the entire spectrum of the profession.

My aim in this book is to examine consulting from as many relevant perspectives as possible, using four recurring approaches which are identified in the text:

- 🏛 A *reflection* – a deeper contemplation of the consulting profession, which is less directly related to the argument and elaborates it.
- 📖 An *example* – a true story, either from literature or from my own practice, in which case the names have been changed.
- 📷 A *case study* – also a true story from my own practice, in which the names have been changed, but explained in more detail and including reflection by the main client concerned in the example.
- 🎥 A *consultant at work* – a brief email interview with a well-known consultant who has a specialism relevant to the chapter in question.
- 🎵 The *summary* at the end of each chapter briefly restates the main themes and definitions in that chapter.

---

1   See the *Ethica Nicomachaea* (Aristotle, 4th century BC).

I would like to say a few words about the illustrations used in this book. The picture on the dust jacket is of a bronze statue of Poseidon from Egina, dating from the second half of the 5th century BC, i.e. towards the end of the "archaic" or Doric period, the era in which the Attic tragedy also reached its peak. Greek culture from this era has, in my view, made the greatest contributions towards the profession of consulting – and has given us wonderful "consultant icons", e.g. in the form of the seers Calchas, Tiresias and Cassandra and of the choruses in many tragedies. All 12 illustrations by Selma van Vemde relate to a single consulting conversation. The epilogue also devotes several pages to the transcription of no more than 20 minutes from a single consulting conversation. What I am trying to convey there is that, as far as I am concerned, the entire content of the book relates to *every* consulting conversation and indeed to *every* moment in consulting. The whole book is in fact a long unravelling of the "here and now" as experienced by myself as consultant.

I would like to thank a number of people who have made crucial contributions towards the line of thought and the world of experience from which this book has evolved. First, all of the different clients and sponsors involved, because it is from my clients that I learn the most, even things that I am not at all keen to learn. The three longer case studies were read through by the three main clients in those consulting projects. Second, a number of fellow professionals who have contributed valuable insights: Sandra Benschop (consultant at FunktieMediair), Jan Jacobs (organisation consultant at De Galan & Voigt), Kathleen King (organisation consultant at Ashridge Consulting), Gertjan Schuiling (independent management consultant), Ineke Sluiter (professor of Greek language and literature at the University of Leiden), Gerard Wijers (director of the Instituut voor Beroepskeuze- en Loopbaanpsychologie), and the consultants interviewed: Andrew Campbell (Ashridge Strategic Management Centre), Roger Harrison (retired independent consultant) and Erica Koch (independent consultant). I would also like to thank Andrew Day, Natasha Molnár (Ashridge Consulting) and Judy Curd (Ashridge Psychometric Services) for their help with the statistics associated with the *Consulting Roles Questionnaire* (see Appendix B). My *action learning group* at Ashridge Consulting, consisting of my colleagues Howard Atkins, Robert Dickson, Laszlo Sabjanyi and Janet Smallwood, has helped me during two "action learning slots" to complete Chapter 10. The help of two other colleagues, Nico Swaan (independent consultant) and Andrew Wilson (Ashridge Centre for Business and Society), has been essential in bringing this English translation towards publication.

I would like to end by expressing the wish that, if this book itself is a piece of advice to the reader, it will not share the fate of many other pieces of advice, namely to be applied unquestioningly. I hope my readers will make up their own minds about our fascinating profession and will choose their own approach. I shall be very pleased to hear about your choices and share your experiences!

Erik de Haan
erik.dehaan@ashridge.org.uk
http://home.hetnet.nl/~e.de.haan

Prologue: Characteristics of Consulting

This book is the result of many reflections on the profession of consulting. My aim is to present those reflections clearly, in the form of summaries of relevant characteristics of consulting, examples and applications. To do so, I make use of a breakdown of the consulting process in time, as found in Bell & Nadler (1979), Block (1981), Kubr (1996) and many others:

1. The entry phase;
2. The diagnosis phase;
3. The implementation phase;
4. The consolidation phase;
5. The evaluation phase.

I have used this classification before myself, in De Haan (2004a). The *odd* chapters of this book give a summary of characteristics of the consulting process in these successive phases. The *even* chapters that follow them contain a deeper reflection. As a result, this book gives the impression that consulting is very much a straightforward profession, although I am addressing precisely those consultants who have learned in their practice that consulting is not as straightforward and unambiguous as the manuals suggest. My target audience is therefore primarily consultants who, through bitter experience, have developed a modest to tragic perspective on the outcome of their interventions.

I define consulting[1] as *a temporary collaborative relationship between a client or client organisation and a consultant, the objective of which is an improvement in the client's fortunes.* The profession of consultant is therefore that of *helpful outsider*, another name which I will sometimes use for the consultant. This definition gives the art of consulting a set

---

1 For a number of alternative definitions, see Appendix A.

of boundaries in time and therefore a well-defined beginning, middle and end. It also gives it a certain directionality, namely "on the path to improvement". In short, it turns consulting into a *process*, a process that can be divided up into phases, as above. These and other phases will be discussed in the coming chapters. But first a warning: when we speak in terms of "consulting process" and "process consulting", and when we distinguish different subdivisions within those concepts, we risk losing sight of other aspects of consulting. It is as with time itself according to St. Augustine: "I know well enough what it is, provided that nobody asks me; but if I am asked what it is and try to explain, I am baffled" (St. Augustine, 398 AD). And when he tries to explain it nevertheless, he concludes a few pages further on: ". . . neither the past nor the future exists; they exist in the mind at present, but nowhere else that I can see".

In my view, therefore, consulting is much more like a *state of mind* in the present than a *process* in time. This state of mind comprises five aspects or main components of consulting. In each of the five odd-numbered chapters that follow, one particular aspect comes to the fore. There seems to be a natural progression within the five, where each seems to be a natural continuation of the one before and so links up closely with the relevant phase in the "consulting process". However, this does not mean that each aspect appears in only one phase. On the contrary, in my experience each central aspect of consulting that I discuss by chapter or by phase is an important theme of consulting at *every* moment.

Most of the experienced consultants who have already read this book have struggled with the description of consulting in several phases and the resulting impression of linearity. In their practice, they have learned not to see that classification into phases as a straitjacket, and not to structure their own contribution as linear and incremental, but rather as an encounter and a joint process of discovery. In addition, they have often experimented with the sequence of phases, for example by deferring the exploration and bringing forward the implementation or evaluation. I thoroughly agree with them, so, when I refer nonetheless to "phases of a consulting process" in the odd-numbered chapters below, I am not referring to the sequence of interventions but to the inevitable passage of time in a time-bound relationship. This underlying advance of time remains an inescapable reality of consulting. Many

modern dramatists, from Beckett onwards, have dispensed with tradi-
tional phasing and the linear passage of time in their works but cannot
get around the fact that their works have a beginning, middle and end.
If only because the public needs to know approximately when to turn
up at the theatre and to have confidence that the evening will not go
on indefinitely. The same is true of management consultancy: despite
heroic attempts to relocate the end at the beginning, to design a
circular process or to give the process "free rein", every consulting
relationship still turns out, over and over again, to be a time-bound
collaboration with a beginning, a middle and an end. I wonder whether
those consultants who have trouble with phasing the passing of
time might really have trouble with saying goodbye or with finitude
in life.

The different aspects to be discussed are as follows:

(in Chapter 1)	Consulting is *fearless speech*: open and honest, without fear of the consequences.
(in Chapter 3)	Consulting is *exploring*: listening to and interpreting whatever the client brings.
(in Chapter 5)	Consulting is *self-monitoring and self-directing*: examining and guiding consulting itself from a different, sometimes more objective, perspective.
(in Chapter 7)	Consulting is *facilitating change*: being present during change, respecting the autonomous nature of change.
(in Chapter 9)	Consulting is *letting go* and leaving to the client what belongs to the client, practising detachment *vis-à-vis* the change that, as a consultant, one has personally become involved in.

Some readers may have noticed that "giving advice" is not part of my
five main aspects of consulting. This is deliberate: in my view, the
actual giving of advice forms only a small and indeed negligible part
of most consulting assignments.

So how does one enter this state of mind that is consulting? The short
answer is by being open to and noticing what is going on with this

client at every moment in this relationship. As I have already said, I believe that consulting actually exists only in the here and now, at this moment. If I can be truly involved in what is going on at present with my client, I have already done most of the "consulting work" for this moment. Consulting begins and ends with a joint focus by client and consultant on improving the situation of one of them, the client.

This *primary task* of the consultant ("being open to and noticing what is going on with this client at every moment in this relationship") which is directed towards the right state of mind for consulting, can be recognised in a number of specialist fields, each of which has a long and distinguished history:

- Vipassana meditation, the oldest form of meditation in Buddhism, which was committed to writing from an oral tradition in the first century BC (see, among others, Walshe, 1987). The aim of Vipassana or insight meditation is to *note* at every moment what is happening at that moment, and then to be able to let it go as you move on to the next moment. For an introduction to Vipassana, see Ahir (1999).

- Hermeneutics, one of the oldest sciences, which developed in Greece in the fifth century BC around the interpretation of older mythological texts. The aim of hermeneutics is to *interpret* human statements, to study stories and texts. Of relevance to consulting is the *hermeneutic circle*, which states that, in order to be able to interpret something, you must already be in the possession of interpretations. For example, you cannot understand the whole without seeing the parts and you cannot understand the parts without seeing the whole. Hermeneutics also teaches that every understanding has a pre-understanding or bias, so that consulting never takes place on the basis of a *tabula rasa*. Schleiermacher (1805–1833) was the first person to view this hermeneutic circle as something problematic.

- Psychoanalysis, the oldest form of psychotherapy, developed in the last decade of the nineteenth century. The psychoanalyst's endeavour is to *note* what is taking place at every moment in the conversation between analyst and patient. For a brief introduction to the primary task in psychoanalysis, with attention to the historical background, see Freud (1920) and, for a description of the consulting profession from a psychoanalytical perspective, see Czander (1993).

Relations between buddhism, hermeneutics, psychoanalysis, research in the social sciences and organisational change have also been highlighted by Bentz & Shapiro (1998). Even though meditators and hermeneuticists do not relate to a client or sponsor and the psychoanalyst does not give advice in principle, I will nevertheless return to the links with these disciplines in the following chapters.

Due to its straightforward classifications and the proliferation of definitions, this book gives the impression that consulting is usually straightforward and well understood while, in my experience, that is often not the case at all. Very often in my practice I do *not* understand what consulting means at this moment, and what is now, at this moment, the best form of consulting. Often I am left wondering: how do I relate to *this* client, at *this* moment? It is precisely this monumental struggle with what is going on, with whom it is going on and what can be done about it that constitutes, at least for me, the vast majority of consulting. Nevertheless, I have adopted a slightly misleading, straightforward structure, precisely in order to create space for a discussion of more sensitive aspects of consulting. In the Epilogue I demonstrate what all of this means in day-to-day practice, with an account of 20 virtually random minutes from a randomly chosen consulting conversation. This example shows that consulting may not be straightforward or well understood, but that we can nevertheless recognise many of the definitions, models and themes from the rest of the book.

1
Characteristics of the Entry

In the first phase of consulting, usually called the "contact and contract phase" (see, for example, Bell & Nadler, 1979), *the establishment of a consulting relationship* can be viewed as the underlying objective. In this phase, the most important question is whether it is possible to achieve the kind of collaborative relationship that is needed for consulting to begin.

Experience shows that the entry usually "begins before it begins": both the client and the consultant have images and expectations of the other person right from the outset, even before they meet. Both the client's organisation and the consultant's profession – and in some cases the client's profession and the consultant's organisation – bring with them such powerful associations that a truly open-minded and unbiased start turns out to be impossible. In consulting, there is no such thing as a "neutral beginning". Let us consider the analogy of going to the theatre to watch a play: before we enter the theatre, we have usually heard a great deal about the play, discussed it with friends, perhaps even read the play, or a review. When the curtain is raised and the initial contact with the performance occurs, we are not unbiased and open-minded but literally full of expectation. Something similar applies in consulting: we already know who the person we are speaking with is, have heard something about him, or have discussed the potential new assignment with colleagues.

For the consultant, the art of intervening and finding out what belongs to the client and what belongs to the consultant (see also Chapter 5) starts from the very first contact. In the first conversation with the client, the consultant is often struck by:

- the sudden profusion of information, both in words and in non-verbal signals;
- the fact that he is suddenly dealing with a problem and a (potential) client at the same time, i.e. with a simultaneous presentation of problem and problem owner;
- the fact that clients often communicate problem and solution at the same time, i.e. they say not only what is bothering them but also what they think should be done about it;
- the complexity of the problem, with a range of interconnected and sometimes contradictory aspects, many of which are only communicated indirectly;
- the reciprocal assessment that often takes place unwittingly, in which the client assesses the consultant for reliability, personality, expertise and experience; and the consultant assesses the client for reliability, features of the problem and relationship to the problem and other relevant parties;
- the difficulty in remaining "authentic" for both client and consultant, in view of the amount of "impression management" that the situation favours.

Despite all of these tensions, each of which places its own demands on the consultant, he attempts to approach the situation as neutrally as possible, trying to free himself from preconceptions and biases, as well as from any self-serving desire to move on to the next phase. Examples of open questions that, asked in a neutral tone, would be useful starting points for the conversation are:
- What can I do for you?
- What brings you here?
- What shall we discuss?
- Where would you like to begin?

The consultant will then attempt to listen, summarise and structure.

Consulting usually starts before it starts: both client and consultant have images and expectations of the other person right from the outset, even before they meet.

Generally speaking, people only ask for advice when they know deep down that they cannot cope on their own. That is why tension is high from the very first moment of contact. Often, the (formal) responsibility of the person we meet is high, while his insight into the origin and development of the problem is still low. We encounter not only the person seeking advice, but also the problem, which, in words and actions, is still indistinguishable from the person. Moreover, it is unlikely that the entire problem will be put on the table at this point: the client may have many reasons not to disclose all the relevant issues yet.

A successful first contact allows the consultant to draw up a contract. The contract boils down to:
- (administrative) a mutual agreement on an initial description of the request and the proposal, preferably at a sufficiently abstract level, keeping open as many options as possible;
- (psychological) a mutual commitment by client and consultant to work towards improvement;
- (professional) conditions which are necessary in order to get a successful collaboration off the ground, especially in terms of mutual responsibilities and roles.

The contract mainly lists the responsibilities of each party.[1] For instance, the consultant undertakes to provide a problem analysis and an improvement plan, and the client offers cooperation in terms of sharing information and displaying a genuine readiness to change limiting conditions and implement changes. Besides this division of responsibilities, both parties are responsible for the fate of third parties. Some contracts may, cruelly, seal the fate of others in the organisation or of a particular department which is performing inadequately in the eyes of the client. Both consultant and client can seek to change the contract, but this may lead to a strong reaction in the other party. The real art is to keep options open in the contracting phase.

In this first phase, if all goes well, the path is cleared for "consulting". As we will see in the next chapter, consulting is not a form of rhetoric, and it is not flattery. Consulting can be most closely associated with "fearless speech", also known as "being authentic" (Block, 1981) or *parrhesia* (Foucault, 1983): the pure form of speech used by philosophers in the presence of kings. Fearless speech is particularly crucial at the start of a consulting journey because the relationship between consultant and client is not yet established and it takes courage to speak fearlessly with someone who is relatively unknown to you. If the consultant can muster the courage to speak fearlessly right from the outset, he clears the path for an open and direct consulting relationship. Consulting often starts with a summary of what the client introduces, which can feel risky enough if the client's emotions and approach towards his problem are also summarised.

In the next chapter I look at the moment when the consultant opens his mouth for the first time and says something about the client's situation, in the form of a summary, impression or advice. How can a consultant handle the client and the client's problem in an authentic manner? And, conversely, under what circumstances does the consultant feel tempted to adopt a less authentic approach?

---

1   In Chapter 8 I examine in greater depth the concept of responsibility and its significance for consulting.

♪ **Summary of characteristics of the entry**

> **Consulting** is a temporary collaborative relationship between client and consultant, the objective of which is an improvement in the client's fortunes.
>
> Consulting is also an attitude or state of mind on the part of the consultant, which takes the following forms:
> 1. **fearless speech**: open and honest, without fear of the consequences;
> 2. **exploration**: listening to and interpreting what the client introduces;
> 3. **self-monitoring and self-directing**: the ability to examine and direct the consulting activity itself from a different, sometimes more objective, perspective;
> 4. **facilitating change**: being present during change, respecting the autonomous nature of change;
> 5. **letting go** of what belongs to the client, practising detachment *vis-à-vis* the change that, as a consultant, one has become personally involved in.

In the first phase, that of the **entry**, the first **contact** and **contracting**, the art of consulting appears to consist primarily in being sufficiently bold to approach the client fearlessly from the very first meeting.

There is no such thing as a neutral **entry**, due to the existing preconceptions of both parties.

During the first **contact** it is often noticeable that:
- problem and problem owner present themselves simultaneously, and so are difficult to distinguish;
- fearless speech comes under pressure straight away, due to the good impression that the consultant – and the client – wants to create.

A **consulting contract** generally contains the following:
- An initial description of the problem, with options for an approach;
- An expression of a mutual commitment to work towards change;
- Conditions which are necessary in order to get a successful consulting relationship off the ground.

2
The Entry and Fearless Speech

But first I would learn whether I may speak freely of
what is going on there, or if I should trim my words.
I fear your hastiness, my lord, your anger, your too potent royalty.

(Euripides, *The Bacchae*, around 406 BC)

Communicating advice

In communicating the advice, the consultant enters the domain of argumentation theory, an age-old disciple that dates back to the art of oratory that was practised intensively as long ago as the ancient Greeks and Romans. Viewed through the lens of argumentation theory, it is clear that communicating as a consultant is no easy matter.

In this chapter I want to consider what communicating advice means within the relationship between consultant and client. What can put this relationship under pressure? How can the relationship itself pose an obstacle to effective communication? Starting with a broad classification, I then go on to examine the main pitfalls in the actual giving of advice within that classification.

Four forms of argumentation

In the broadest sense, I distinguish four different intentions in speech. These intentions lead to four forms of argumentation, as follows:

- First, there is the intention to *advocate and reason*, and to convince others of a particular viewpoint. The aim here is to win the other person around to your point of view, or to motivate others to do something. The respective positions of the speakers may differ. There are certain professions where this form of argumentation is widely used, such as those of the politician and the lawyer.
- Second, there is the intention of "pure" *conversation*, the intention to arrive at as thorough and clear as possible an understanding in a discussion of questions and answers. The speakers are in principle equals, they ask a lot of questions, listen carefully and attempt to

rise above personal interests. The conversation or dialogue proceeds via all sorts of pros and cons, viewing them from different perspectives and making use of a range of distinctions and explanations, progressing gradually towards a conclusion that is satisfactory for all participants.

- Third, there is the intention of *fearless speech*, the intention to express in a personal and open manner, without personal interest and irrespective of the wishes or direct interests of the other person, how the speaker himself sees things or feels. This speech intention becomes a challenge if there is a marked difference in status or power between the speaker and the person he is addressing. Fearless speech is relatively easy between equals and if the issues discussed are not of a delicate or sensitive nature, but it can be a real act of bravery if it takes place within the relationship between an adviser and a person in power or if a sensitive issue is on the agenda.
- Fourth, there is the intention of *flattery*, the intention to say precisely those things that the other person wants to hear, irrespective of one's own opinion and irrespective of the truth. The aim here is to make the other person feel better. To flatter, it is necessary to make an accurate assessment of what the other person wants to hear, or what he feels unsure or sensitive about. Flattery can take place between people of any status.

A reflection: the four forms of argumentation in ancient Athens

Although the subdivision in four forms of argumentation as presented in this chapter does not exist in ancient writings about the subject, each of the forms of argumentation has a clear predecessor in Greek philosophy:

1. In ancient Greece, and later in Rome as well, particular importance was attached to the art of oratory and advocacy, or *rhetorica*. The *rhetor* was a man of distinction who carried a lot of weight in both political and legal circles. Free men with ambition were therefore trained intensively in rhetoric. Many guides written in this field still survive. One of the most comprehensive is that of Quintilianus (around 94 AD). Great orators were celebrated because they could make you believe anything, were reputed to be able to win virtually any legal case and commanded a great deal of respect in public meetings or the senate.

2. The Greeks called the art of conversation *dialectics*, the art of conducting a dialogue properly. Plato (4th century BC) described dialectics and sang its praises as a genuine method of arriving at the right point of view, the right intention and the right decision. See, for example, his dialogue *The Sophist*, which is both constructed purely dialectically and deals largely with dialectics.

3. An expert in the art of fearless speech or *parrhesia* was Diogenes of Sinope, the renowned "cynic" or literally "dog-like" philosopher, who shocked people with his outrageous statements and behaviour. It was he who told Alexander the Great, when the latter came to pay his respects, not to stand between him and the sun. We also read that he masturbated in a market square full of people, "because surely one may also meet other physical needs there, such as eating and drinking". References to the art of fearless speech are found in Euripides and Lucianus among others (see Foucault, 1983).

4. The Greeks rarely have anything positive to say about the art of flattery or *kolakia*, but there are many warnings against it, such as that by the famous orator Isocrates (355 BC). Isocrates fulminates against flatterers and sycophants, whom he accuses of confusing their listeners and bringing misfortune upon them.

Other classifications are also employed in rhetoric.[1] In this classification, which I believe can be applied very usefully to the profession of consulting, I have brought together two less well-known forms of argumentation (fearless speech and flattery) and two better-known forms (advocating and conversing). In two of these four forms of argumentation, the truth is central as far as possible (conversing and fearless speech): the first case concerns a shared or, sometimes, "objective" truth and the second case a more personal or "subjective" truth. In the other two forms (advocacy and flattery) the effect of the argumentation on the listener is central. Advocacy and fearless speech have in common the fact that they usually meet with opposition and, as a result, sometimes change into conversation or flattery.

---

1 See, for example, Foss *et al.* (1985). Since Plato in particular, there have been many attempts to categorise all of these forms of argumentation within dialectics and, since Aristotle, within rhetoric.

	Greek term:	Strives for:	Makes use of:	Is pre-eminently suitable for:
Reasoning and advocacy	*Rhetorica*	Persuasiveness	Proposals, reasons, arguments, proof	Politicians, lawyers, managers (among themselves)
Conversing	Dialectics	Finding the truth	Shared facts and opinions, summaries	Scientists, philosophers (among themselves)
Fearless speech	*Parrhesia*	Candour	Personal opinions	Advisers (to managers), managers (to higher managers)
Flattery	*Kolakia*	A good feeling	Compliments, inspiration	No one really, or perhaps some salesmen (to customers)

A different summary can be given in terms of aspects which are central in communication and is as follows:[2]

Directed towards impact on the other person

Advocacy	**Flattery**

Objective ——————————————————— Personal

Conversation	**Fearless speech**

Directed towards authenticity and truthfinding

---

2   William Isaacs (1999), on the basis of his research into different ways of "thinking together", proposes a model that bears some similarities to this diagram. He refers to four different stages of development of dialogues, as follows:
   1.   Polite and conventional conversations, characterised by predictable etiquette and flattery;

Forms of argumentation for consultants

Let me emphasise that every consultant uses all four forms of argumentation at different times. During entry, orientation and conducting research, a specific form of conversing is always used. In presenting an investigative report or the possibilities and limitations of one's own service as consultant, a form of reasoning or advocating is often used. And which of us can be sure that we never flatter our clients, on first meeting them for example, when we hear about a new, intriguing problem, a problem that tempts us, or later, due to our own uncertainty or need to be liked? Moreover, the boundaries between "positive" or "supportive" feedback and flattery are extremely blurred.

A reflection: the consultant without power of persuasion

In order to understand that we need power of persuasion as a consultant, we need only consider perhaps the most tragic consultant from classical mythology: Cassandra, the daughter of Priamus and Hecabe. She was the prophet who always spoke the truth about the future, but without any power of persuasion. Apollo gave her the gift of predicting the future in exchange for the promise of sexual favours. When she backed out at the last minute, he put a curse on her that cancelled out her gift completely: no one would ever believe her. For example, Cassandra later warned her fellow citizens of Troy about the soldiers hiding in the Trojan horse, but no one took heed of her warning. For consultants, the story of Cassandra is a warning to maintain close contact with the client and to investigate first whether someone is prepared to listen to us, before we bring our "wisdom" into play.

Conversing, advocating and flattering are therefore relevant to consultants at different times but, in my experience, fearless speech is the form of argumentation best suited to the role of consultant, especially where the objective is to achieve genuine benefits for clients under fairly difficult conditions. Fearless speech is also one of the main

---

2. Controlled discussions infused with friction, characterised by advocating and debating;
3. Investigative dialogue, characterised by exploration and conversation;
4. Generative dialogue, characterised by fearless speech and creativity.

These stages can also be identified in the diagram above and run from personal and directed towards impact to personal and directed towards authenticity.

expectations that clients have of their consultants, albeit often implicitly. In codes of conduct for management consultants, such as those of the British Institute of Management Consultancy, the Canadian Association of Management Consultants or the US Association of Management Consulting Firms, the consultant's *independence* is put central from the very start. The Dutch code of conduct for management consultants, drawn up by the professional associations ROA and Ooa, starts with general rules and then immediately broaches the subject of independence, stating (in point 2.1) that: "The consultant shall not accept an assignment if he is not given the opportunity to form his own, independent opinion and to convey it to his client." So right from the outset of most codes of conduct, fearless speech assumes a central position.

An example

Fearless speech can also be important for managers, especially when talking to senior management. I am frequently in conversation with managers and recommend *parrhesia* to them, for example when they harbour criticisms of their own managers. Often, they have not yet expressed the criticisms directly themselves but do want to share them with me as their consultant. On my part, it is an act of fearless speech to state that it is not very productive to say this to the consultant, but not to your manager.

In such situations I often encounter unspoken expectations in managers: the expectation that I, as the consultant, will go and "sort things out" with senior management or at least report "spontaneously" to them in some form or another, while preserving confidentiality and therefore speaking purely on my own account. These are upsetting expectations because, in the first instance, they bring the consulting to an end or, in the second instance, the communication is taking place through me, so that I am only helping to weaken direct communication within the organisation.

The fearless consultant

On account of its evident importance for consultants, I would like to deepen the examination of fearless speech or *parrhesia*. I am following Foucault's 1983 lecture cycle on this topic (Foucault, 1983). He mentions a number of characteristics of *parrhesia*:
1. Practising *parrhesia* I say what I think about the other person – it therefore involves a personal and sincere opinion on what I see or encounter.

2. Practising *parrhesia* I experience a difference in status or responsibility between myself as speaker and my audience, where I am "lower" than my audience in those respects.
3. Practising *parrhesia* I say something that is risky or dangerous for me.
4. Practising *parrhesia* I am also at liberty to remain silent – fearless speech is therefore a personal role interpretation for me; no one forces me to do it.

On the basis of these points Foucault concludes that a person who is speaking fearlessly should possess certain moral qualities, such as integrity and courage. Examples are when you say to your tyrannical boss that his tyranny is disturbing or unpleasant, or when you risk incurring the wrath of friends by telling them what mistakes you think they are making. You prefer to see yourself as a "speaker of your own truth" rather than as someone who is untruthful to himself, and are prepared to pay a price for this distinction, in the form of putting your relationship with others at risk. There is also a socially inappropriate form of *parrhesia*, where you keep saying what you think without imposing any restraints, so that you come across as a sort of annoying, egocentric chatterbox.

A reflection: the parrhesiastic contract

The Greeks were very interested in the ways in which kings handle their advisers. Was the king able to join in the game of *parrhesia*? How did he react when the adviser spoke fearlessly? The king was called a tyrant if he punished his advisers for it, while a good king tolerated everything said to him by an adviser speaking fearlessly. Foucault (1983) talks about a sort of *parrhesiastic contract*, which still embodies the essence of consulting today: the sovereign, the one who has power but lacks truth, addresses himself to the one who has truth but lacks power, and tells him: "If you tell me the truth, no matter what this truth turns out to be, you won't be punished." In philosophy, *parrhesia* was connected with concern for oneself (see also Foucault, 1984): by speaking fearlessly, the philosopher alerts others, namely ambitious young men and leaders, to the importance of care or concern for oneself.[3] The topic of "advising powerful leaders" is again examined in Chapter 6.

---

3 See also Foucault's definition of advice in Appendix A.

The fearless consultant sometimes finds it necessary to question the original formulation of the problem: "This is a just lot of old flannel as far as I am concerned – so what is really going on here?"

The four characteristics of *parrhesia* are usually present in organisation consultancy: based on his own knowledge, skill and experience, the consultant expresses a personal and subjective opinion. This consultant has no formal status in the organisation and, indeed, is generally in a "lower" and risky position, because, when delivering bad or unwanted news, he might come to stand alone against something that is bigger than him, namely a whole organisation or – in a dialogue – the person who is his client. Finally, despite the fact that clients often pressure consultants to give advice, the decision actually to do so, and when to do so, remains the preserve of the consultant. The consultant is also free at any time to remain silent: all giving of advice takes place on the basis of his own concept of role, which says: "Here and now I should speak fearlessly and give my opinion or advice."

Some examples

Here are four consultancy situations from my own practice. Which form of argumentation appears most suitable here? And what are the risks of that approach? My own responses in these situations are given in the footnote on the following page.

Case 1

This case involves a staff department of a university. Our client, the head of department, requests some follow-up training on project management for the department, because it is still not being applied sufficiently. We conduct exploratory interviews with 10 consultants from the department. Almost unanimously, they express a critical view of their own manager, our client, whom they accuse of showing too little involvement and at the same time checking details of projects in a bureaucratic manner. Before we start to write our interview report, we have one more interview to conduct, with our client.

Case 2

This case took place in a factory where I was conducting research into the working relationships within the quality control department. Those relations proved to be extremely mistrustful and destructive, so my advice was to transfer a number of people. This advice was not followed by my client, the factory director, but it did create a lot of emotional turmoil in the department. The client asked me to work together with the department to bring about improvements, while retaining all of the staff concerned.

Case 3

In the directorate of a large government institution, all 40 policy workers there had attended a course on coaching skills a few years before. As a follow-up to that course, they asked us to facilitate peer consultation groups, to enable them to recall what they had learned and practise it more intensively. After a number of interviews, we gained the impression that more was needed, namely a common focus on the part of everyone involved within the directorate.

Case 4

The three depots of a local transportation company are not working together enough. There is a great deal of rivalry and a close solidarity between employees working from the same depot, a solidarity which is often greater than the solidarity felt with the organisation as a whole. I am invited to chair a working conference in which the problems will be talked through and new arrangements will be made for the future. In the preparatory discussions before the conference, I get the impression that these colleagues have a lot of opinions about each other that they do not express to each other, but do express to me.[4]

Fearless speech under pressure

In practice there is a huge temptation for consultants to resort to other forms of argumentation, such as advocacy or flattery, even where this actually stops the consulting process dead. We all know the example of the consultant who believes so fervently in his own advice that he will move heaven and earth to persuade the client to adopt it. Or the consultant who is so enthralled with his own models and tools that he never stops talking about them. In both cases the consulting is actually over; the consultant is more concerned with himself than with the client. We also know the examples of consultants who continue to give the client positive feedback, even where this is no longer effective, and consultants who want to spare the client's feelings or lack the courage to deliver bad news that might anger him.

I believe that fearless speech – and fearless writing, where appropriate – forms the essence of a consultant's communication. It is therefore important to examine where the consultant might be tempted to dilute, cover up or abandon his fearless speech. This temptation is of course all the greater where clients have more power over the consultant or the consultant is less certain, for example about his own opinion or his own relationship to the client. In my experience, fearless speech comes under pressure in the following circumstances:

---

4   In the four situations described, I tried the following forms of argumentation:
1. Fearless speech. The main risk of *parrhesia* was apparent here: the client was very deeply affected, did say that she wouldn't blame the messenger for "bringing bad news", but gradually became cooler towards us and ended the relationship within a few weeks.
2. Conversing, because the time for fearless speech is over. I was honoured with a difficult follow-up assignment, due to all of the internal opposition to my report, and was at the same time settled in well enough to be able to tackle it energetically and dialectically.
3. Reasoning, because our point of view was opposed to that of the client. We explained our view as convincingly as possible and, after doing so, were asked to map out a broader programme with a common starting point, with the aim of creating the focus to get down to work.
4. Fearless speech, both in the preliminary discussions and during the conference. This fearless speech during the conference left the participants free, as far as possible, to speak to each other more fearlessly. Interventions of the type: "I have the impression that there is more going on here", "It seems to me that you are pussyfooting around."

- When the consultant is intimidated by the client and no longer "dares" to be fearless;
- Where the consultant's involvement with his client or his own advice becomes so strong and unbending that it becomes fossilised;
- Where the consultant's motivation to speak freely decreases because his involvement is very low;
- On account of – often unconscious – needs of the consultant to be thought "likeable" or "competent" above all else;
- On account of – often unconscious – needs of the client to hear "good news" or be "supported" above all else.

Due to the impact of (unconscious) needs, the possible loss of fearless speech is closely connected with the personalities of consultant and client. Not every consultant can advise every client, therefore, but the consultant can increase his ability to advise by being more aware of his own needs and deferring the satisfaction of those needs or channelling them differently. This means that the consultant must apply "self-reflection and self-direction" (see Chapter 5), asking questions such as: What are my needs? What are those of my client? What form of communication do I see myself using? and Is it the most appropriate?

Because I have noticed that it is worthwhile to maintain *fearless consulting* under difficult circumstances, I would like to look again at fearless speech under pressure, from a different angle. Which forms of argumentation do consultants sometimes substitute for fearlessness, and when? The reader may recognise the following scenarios:

- I start to *advocate instead of speaking fearlessly*. I see myself doing this when I am very attached to my advice or when I have the impression that a client is not listening to me while I am trying to advise him. Then it may happen that without being aware of it I change over to advocating, reasoning, and even . . . nagging.
- I start to *flatter instead of speaking fearlessly*. This is a huge temptation, especially for successful consultants. They notice that positive feedback is not only valued by many clients, but that such feedback encourages and motivates clients to a large degree. It is very tempting to lower the threshold for positive signals ever further. It is important for a consultant, right from the outset, to be able to

distinguish quite precisely between positive feedback and flattery. The main difference lies, I believe, in the *intention*. If the positive opinion is authentic and expressed fearlessly, we are miles away from flattery. If the same positive opinion is expressed in order to make the other person feel good or to make oneself as consultant more popular, it is dripping with flattery. However, it can be extremely difficult for a client to tell a flatterer from a fearless speaker[5] – they often say the same things and in the same way. Usually, only the consultant himself can judge the difference in

---

5   As is demonstrated clearly by Plutarch's fascinating essay *How to distinguish a flatterer from a friend?* (Plutarch, 109 AD). Plutarch suggests 10 ways to tell a friend from a flatterer, so a "true" from a "false" adviser:
   1. The advice of a flatterer stems from what the other person seems to want to hear, so will generally be less constant and consistent than that of a friend;
   2. The flatterer does not apply a coherent underlying model when giving advice;
   3. The flatterer gives opinions and advice on all sorts of aspects of your actions, virtually indiscriminately – and will often appreciate even your worst traits;
   4. The flatterer makes himself less than an equal – while, conversely, he talks himself up more when it comes to his weaknesses and bad habits;
   5. The candour of a flatterer is often exaggerated because it is not genuine candour;
   6. In his candour, a flatterer will sometimes criticise the opposite of your weakness or mistake – so as to give you an indirect pat on the back;
   7. If a flatterer does something for you, he will often exaggerate it or in any case will always make it abundantly clear that he is indeed doing something for you;
   8. A flatterer will be equally pleased to do small things and large things for you, and will keep checking with you whether he has done it properly;
   9. A flatterer will always agree with your opinion; you can therefore unmask the flatterer by announcing two contradictory opinions within a short space of time (compare with the well-known scene between Hamlet and Polonius [*Hamlet*, III.2.385], where the protagonist keeps seeing new shapes in a cloud and the flatterer immediately concurs with all of them);
   10. A flatterer is keen to be your only friend and therefore tends to be jealous of your other friends – the reverse is true of a friend, because he wants you to have as many friends as possible.
   Despite all of these differences, Plutarch emphasises the great difficulty of trapping a flatterer, because the flatterer is a *professional* who constantly endeavours to cancel out anything that might set him apart from a friend. And a flatterer is also capable of studying the aspects above, and then trying to correct them!

intention and indeed even many consultants find it difficult to recognise an intention to flatter in themselves. One of the indicators that I use in order to recognise an intention to flatter in myself is to note the way in which I think and talk about my clients when they are not around. If it is more negative than when I am talking to them, I have often given in to an intention to flatter.[6]

- *I start to conduct an "ordinary" conversation instead of speaking fearlessly.* I see myself doing this in circumstances in which it seems too painful to express the advice fearlessly, for example just after giving confrontational feedback. The other person may then give all sorts of background to his own behaviour, as it were in order to "explain" or even defend himself, and before you know it the client is drawing you as the consultant into a "congruous" conversation full of chit-chat, where a more objective attitude is more appropriate.

A consultant needs clients and client problems for his own continued existence as a consultant, so there is always a certain susceptibility to invitations to use a way of speaking other than what is most appropriate. Especially if the consultant is not free of narcissism and self-importance, he may be susceptible to flattery: clients praise the consultant to the skies and try to get him to do their dirty work for them. It is striking how much people who flatter are often highly susceptible to flattery themselves. It may therefore be a long and painful chastening process for a consultant to purge himself gradually of the desire to flatter and be flattered, and to learn to *choose* for himself the right way to speak in the particular circumstances.

A consultant at work

Interview with Erica Koch, independent consultant in training and management consulting working under the name *Parrhesia*:

The last part of his essay is an excellent guide to the practice of *parrhesia*: Plutarch examines various methods of adapting fearless speech to the circumstances and measuring it in such a way that it can be heard. Indispensable fare for any consultant!

6   And if I talk more positively about my clients than when I am with them, and realise that, I often discover that I have been overcritical of my clients due to projective identification (Czander, 1993) or my own countertransference (see also Chapter 10 and the Epilogue for an example).

Why did you call your consultancy Parrhesia?
I came into contact with the term *parrhesia* during a philosophy workshop with Jan Flameling in Greece. I was looking for a motto or a guiding principle along which I could develop my work. *Parrhesia* fitted the bill perfectly. The name almost always prompts clients to ask what *parrhesia* means, thereby immediately starting a conversation about something essential.

How important do you think parrhesia, *or "saying everything", or fearless speech, is for a consultant?*
I think a consultant must be able to speak fearlessly, with the sole intention of helping the client. However, that is more easily said than done; in my view it takes courage, but also sensitivity. In any case, I do not think that always saying everything that occurs to you is the ultimate in fearless speech for a consultant. Timing and an understanding of what the other person is able to hear are at least as important.

The fact that I work as an independent consultant makes it easier for me to speak fearlessly. I do not feel any responsibility for the interests of my firm or the growth of our business, I only have my own responsibility.

Who are most capable of parrhesia, *and what training do you recommend in order to develop* parrhesia *further?*
Difficult question. I sometimes think that only young children are really capable of *parrhesia* – they are still so uninhibited and lack the hesitation or reserve that I sometimes feel. I suspect that a consultant who is employed in order to achieve a result that has been discussed previously feels less free. I don't know of any specific training to develop *parrhesia*, but I think reflection and maintaining a dialogue with your clients and colleagues is one way of developing your own fearless thinking and speech. Peer consultation with colleagues and clear feedback from my clients are important aids for me. Argyris' body of ideas (see, for example, Argyris & Schön, 1978) also helps me enormously.

When do you notice that parrhesia *is put to the test, or becomes hard to maintain?*
It becomes difficult when there are a lot of different interests at stake, especially when I myself feel that I have to defend an interest. It becomes more difficult for me if my role or contribution comes under discussion and I start to feel uncertain about my role as a result. It is sometimes difficult to keep communicating fearlessly about those feelings and to keep a clear distinction between what has to do with myself and what has to do with the client's system.

Conclusion

Finally, let us take one last look at the differences between the four forms of argumentation, with the aid of a familiar example. Suppose one of our friends asks our advice on how to give up smoking. The following four possible reactions illustrate the differences:

1. *Advocating*: "Let's keep a close eye on it. Give me your remaining cigarettes and agree with me that you won't touch another cigarette from now on. I'll check up on you regularly."
2. *Conversing*: "There are various ways of stopping smoking. Which have you tried already? And what was the result? What do you now think is the best way, for you?"
3. *Fearless speech*: "You've been smoking for so long that I can hardly imagine you without a cigarette. I can't do much to help you – you'll really have to rely on yourself here."
4. *Flattery*: "What a brave thing for you to do. I can hardly imagine you without a cigarette, and it's always suited you so well. Surely smoking isn't as unhealthy as they say. But if you want to try to stop, you have my full support. You can do it: I believe in you."

We can imagine fearless speech at the mid-point of a straight line with "bluntness" and "flattery" at the extremes. The consultant attempts to achieve mastery by staying away from these extremes and feeling comfortable in the middle zone, applying fearless speech in a variety of situations.

♪

Summary: fearless consulting

I distinguish four intentions to speech, leading to four **forms of argumentation** or methods of communication as a consultant:

- **Reasoning and advocating** or **rhetoric**: making proposals, putting forward arguments and furnishing proof;
- **Conversing** or **dialectics**: sharing facts and opinions, listening and building on each other's comments in order to arrive at a joint conclusion;
- **Fearless speech** or **parrhesia**: contributing personal opinions in a relaxed and confident manner;
- **Flattery** or **kolakia**: saying what the other person wants to hear; conveying compliments, confidence and "a good feeling" in an inspiring manner.

Good consulting under difficult circumstances is, above all, fearless speech. **Fearless speech** involves:

1. saying what you think and mean;
2. even though it may be risky or dangerous for you as the speaker;
3. from a lower status or a position of lesser responsibility;
4. from your own free will and your own interpretation of your role as consultant.

Flattery, of the four forms of argumentation, is perhaps the most harmful for the consulting relationship.

When is it difficult to maintain fearless consulting?

- A feeling of intimidation (consultant);
- Strong and unbending involvement in one's own opinion (consultant);
- Too little involvement resulting in inadequate motivation (consultant);
- (Unconscious) need to be liked and thought competent (consultant);
- (Unconscious) need for support and good news (client).

3
Characteristics of Joint Problem Formulation

In this second phase of the consulting assignment, the consultant elaborates further on the first contact and the contract. The aim of consulting now appears to be *to explore further what the issue is which is presented for consulting*. The consultant has managed to establish a collaborative relationship with the client which paves the way for consulting. This can have happened within a fraction of a second, of course, but sometimes it may require an extensive, protracted contracting period. The consultant's attention is now focused on charting and exploring the issues, tasks which were also part of the first phase.

Similar to the establishment of a consulting relationship in the first phase, the exploration phase therefore seems to "start before it starts". During the initial contact the consultant was already gathering first impressions and he was involved in initial formulations of the problem. Now these impressions will become richer and more diverse as the consultant meets and interviews other stakeholders and hears other, perhaps even irreconcilable, formulations of the problem. There is therefore a gradual transition from entry to exploration.

If the first phase was *working towards* consulting, the second phase is a sort of *suspension* of consulting. It is as if the consulting might start at any time, but has not started yet. In the theatre, this is the time when we are still looking around and taking in our surroundings, studying the décor, the lighting and the actors' costumes and gestures, but have not yet become completely engrossed in their story. Experienced consultants are adept at stretching out this expectation that there is something brewing, that something is about to happen, sometimes to such an extent that deferment leads to abandonment: they manage *never* to give any advice and yet achieve all of the desired results of the assignment. After the contracting period there is often already some pressure on the consultant to consult, but consulting still seems premature. One of the difficulties for the consultant is to rid himself of the "assessing" and "judging" impulses which seemed useful or at least unavoidable in the entry phase. In this phase some consultants tend to continue assessing and applying their expertise. They do their best to skip over this phase and offer direct, "straightforward" advice. That may indeed be possible with some "straightforward problems". This phase gains in importance where other points of view are also possible or where the client himself and his attitude or approach are part of the problem.

Exploration is a skill and an activity, but also, like consulting in a broader sense, an intention or state of mind. In my view, every consultant will have his own "exploratory attitude". On the basis of my experience with different consultants in the exploration phase, I can distinguish several different exploratory approaches:

1. The *research attitude*, with a high degree of objectivity and predictability. An example is the consultant with notepad in hand, often with a list of prepared questions that are ticked off one by one.
2. The *diagnostic attitude*, which is strongly oriented towards the symptoms, problems, conflicts and other difficulties. This consultant attempts to chart the problem carefully and objectively.
3. The almost diametrically opposed attitude of *appreciative inquiry*. This consultant seeks primarily to establish what is experienced as positive at present, what is currently working well and what can serve as a basis for future improvement.
4. Pure *exploration*, so simply experiencing "what is there". This consultant attempts to exert as little influence as possible when gathering his information, aiming to put the client at the centre and to listen as closely as possible to what the client is offering.

The choice of approach depends very much on the role for which the consultant has been contracted (for examples, see Chapter 5). For the most difficult and intractable problems, it appears sensible to work on the problem formulation a bit longer and in more depth and to opt, as far as possible, for the fourth approach. The other approaches tend to have an interventional aspect, the consultant already having decided what interests him most. In "research" it is certain predefined categories, in "diagnosis" it is the "bad news" and in "appreciative inquiry" the "good news". In practice, however, it is not easy to embark upon a pure exploration. Opinions, emotions, desires and memories tend to pop up in the consciousness of the consultant, who therefore requires a great deal of training to focus more wholly and consistently on whatever the client brings.

The attentive consultant puts herself in the client's shoes and perceives his world from the inside, so to speak. While exploring, the consultant sometimes resembles a chameleon taking on the colours of the client.

If one looks at the beginnings of different consulting assignments, a feature that they often seem to have in common is an internal contradiction of some kind. All of the issues presented involve something undesirable that the client is finding hard to get rid of, or something desirable that is proving difficult to achieve. It may be a strategy or a practice that has become ingrained and the client is finding hard to shake off, or a change in circumstances that he is finding hard to cope with. The client therefore wants to change something and to remain largely unchanged at the same time. Matching this, we as consultants often feel a degree of ambivalence ourselves in this phase, for example between our need to empathise with the client's problems and our need to observe and study the client's situation from an independent perspective. An ambivalence, therefore, between experiencing the situation as the client experiences it, and at the same time experiencing the situation as an outsider would experience it.

The client, moreover, almost always feels a sort of ambivalence about entering into the consulting relationship. Whether or not he admits it to himself, the client feels that he has virtually been handed over to someone who "knows better" or "deals well with these issues", which puts him in an awkward position of dependency. Whereas, on the one hand, the contract with the consultant contains the promise that a solution or a better approach will be found, the relationship with the consultant entails, on the other hand, the unpleasant connotation of dependence on an outsider, a connotation that the client by no means always registers consciously. In the following chapter we take a closer look at these ambivalences, internal contradictions and ambiguities that virtually always occur in consulting.

Once the consultant has spent some time studying the client and situation, he sometimes experiences a certain inevitability: before the consultant understands exactly how the situation developed, he senses the inescapable patterns that lie at the root of events. "Under those circumstances that issue was *bound* to arise", is the thought that inevitably springs to mind.

Emotions in the client that seemed surprising in the contact phase, such as cynicism or pent-up anger, gradually become understandable and recognisable. For the consultant, it is best not to empathise too greatly with those feelings lest, before he knows it, he is dragged in and has become an insider. And, as an insider, he becomes part of the system, while his expertise has been called in for the very reason that he can examine the system from the vantage point of an independent outsider.

Pressure can come from various sides to "solve the problem". The consultant can also feel pressured to live up to the image of solidity, reliability and expertise that he established in the contact phase. The aim of the exploration is ultimately to change something in the client's situation. However, the consultant may have good grounds for deciding to wait until he is sure he has all of the relevant facts before springing into action.

In the following chapter I look at a specific aspect of exploration by the consultant: being sensitive to ambiguities – in the client's description of or attitude towards the problem, for example. How can a helpful outsider handle subtle, ambivalent issues without offering a personal opinion or giving advice? And what is the effect of summaries that put the client's ambivalence into words?

Summary of characteristics of joint problem formulation

> **Consulting** is a temporary collaborative relationship between client and consultant, the objective of which is an improvement in the client's fortunes.
>
> Consulting is also an attitude or state of mind on the part of the consultant, which takes the following forms:
> 1. **Fearless speech**: open and honest, without fear of the consequences;
> 2. **Exploration**: listening to and interpreting what the client introduces;
> 3. **Self-monitoring and self-directing**: the ability to examine and direct the consulting activity itself from a different, sometimes more objective, perspective;
> 4. **Facilitating change**: being present during change, respecting the autonomous nature of change;
> 5. **Letting go** of what belongs to the client, practising detachment *vis-à-vis* the change that, as a consultant, one has become personally involved in.

In the second phase, that of **joint problem formulation**, the art of consulting appears to consist primarily of making oneself receptive to the client's situation.

Roughly speaking, there are four types of **exploration**:
1. Objective **research**, based on checklists or other tools;
2. **Diagnosis**, examining the problem in all of its manifestations and backgrounds;
3. **Appreciative inquiry**, examining what is working well and what can form a basis for a new approach;
4. Observing and **experiencing** what appears to be relevant.

The client's initial problem is always **ambivalent** in one way or another – and usually in more than one way:
- The client wants to achieve something, to learn how to cope with something or to get rid of something – but doesn't want to give up anything precious in the process;
- The client claims one thing but, at a deeper level, is struggling with something quite different;
- The client has ambivalent feelings towards the consultant, who is welcome as a helper but also less welcome as a (potential) threat to the client's autonomy.

4
Problem Formulation and Irony

*Irony says: "we pretend to know what we are talking about,
and we don't forget for a moment that we're only pretending."*

(Kellendonk, *The feathers of the swan*, 1987)

Ambiguous communication[1]

While exploring a consulting issue, the consultant naturally attempts, above all, to listen to the issues as closely as possible, to ask good questions, to summarise, and to immerse himself as fully as possible in the situation and the client's problem. We have all experienced what it feels like to be sitting opposite a good listener, someone who becomes absorbed, shows understanding and senses what is really going on with us. A good listener is able, with his intuition, to bring to light aspects of the problem of which you yourself are only half aware. As a "good listener", a consultant can therefore open up new perspectives on the problem even during its initial exploration, even without offering his own impressions or advice. It is striking how powerful the effect of good listening can be in this respect.

What an attentive consultant actually does is immerse himself in the internal world or frame of reference of the client. Together with the client, the consultant explores how the problem looks *to the client*. Interestingly, with that sensitivity the good listener automatically becomes receptive to ambiguities and irony:
1. In my experience, clients are virtually always ambivalent about their request for advice: they are keen for that request to be met, but also keen to stay where they are; they therefore want change and no change at the same time.

---

1   An earlier version of this chapter appears in De Haan (1999).

2. Ambivalence may also arise due to differences between the approach currently being undertaken and the description or justification of that approach. Argyris & Schön (1978) show that the two are by no means always the same: our *theory-in-use*, which we *appear* to follow in given circumstances, is by no means always the same as our *espoused theory*, which we *profess* to follow in given circumstances.

3. Finally, there are the types of ambivalence mentioned in Chapter 3 regarding the request for advice in the first place and the search for a consultant. Clients requesting advice are by no means always unambiguous in this respect – for example, they are happy to pursue their request for advice, but at the same time are afraid of the sacrifices that such advice might entail, or of the loss of autonomy.

If the consultant is sensitive to these types of ambivalence and attempts to give a summary of the complete and ambiguous picture, the consultant will frequently and automatically communicate ironically and ambiguously.

Let us take a more general look at personal changes in more or less stable contexts. There is a conviction that something must or could be changed. But while the new is not yet present, the old must already be left behind. This causes pressure for change and, simultaneously, fear of what may come. This creates tension for the person concerned in two conflicting ways.[2] Experience shows that a good listener in the form of a "helpful outsider" can help in such situations:

- The outsider is a new player, but remains largely the same, and thus personifies both aspects of the ambivalence "old/new" which is so important for the client.[3]
- The outsider can reflect on the (proposed) changes.
- The outsider may be able to say something in advance about the forthcoming new situation.

---

2 For more information on the opposing pressures resulting from this "fear of learning" and "fear for survival", see Schein *et al.* (1961) and De Haan (2004b), Chapter 18.

3 Which means that, for the client, the consideration of *this* situation, with *this* outsider, in itself may already be relevant to the implementation of the change, over and above the transference (Freud, 1912a) which also makes the here-and-now relevant for the client.

Whether the outsider is a guide, a teacher, a supplier, a consultant or a therapist, experience shows that his contribution can be helpful in bringing about the proposed change.

Much has been written about the profession of the helpful outsider or consultant (see also the bibliography at the end of this book). It appears to be no easy profession, because it entails a variety of pitfalls:
• Becoming too involved and so no longer being an outsider;
• Choosing an approach that generates resistance and so no longer being helpful;
• Losing the connection and so no longer being effective;
• Taking on too much and so allowing the other person no space for change.

In this chapter I examine irony as a consulting technique for applying ambiguous observations and reflecting those observations back in such a way that the consultant "communicates ambiguously".

I am not seeking possible causes of change, types of change or effects of change. Nor do I attempt to describe the necessary experience of the outsider or the personal experience of change that he should possess. I am only seeking to identify the communicative approach of the helpful outsider which is adopted towards the changing person (or changing organisation), and its effects. I draw in this respect on an article by Visscher and Rip (1999) where, in a typology of management consultants, beside the "enlightened modern" and the "post-modern", they also consider the "ironic type", and on a book by Jonathan Lear (2003) which makes a "sincere plea" in favour of irony as a key technique of the psychotherapist.

What is irony?

Irony comes from the Greek word *eirooneia*, which is probably derived from the verb "eiroo": to say, speak, report.[4] "Saying something that you do not think" was perhaps the original meaning. This means that

---

4   As one might expect with this concept, its etymology is ambiguous. Possibly the derivation is from *eiromai*, to ask. In that case irony originally carried the significance of "probing into new, hidden layers of meaning".

eirooneia was something like feigned ignorance or, conversely, pretend-ing that you know more than you are saying. A well-known form of irony in classical Athens was Socratic irony: Socrates emphasised his own ignorance, which came across to others as "playing the innocent". The first of the *Characters* of Theophrastos (319 BC) was the *ironicos*: a hypocrite who always says the opposite of what he means.

For the purposes of this chapter, I define irony as a figure of speech which is characterised by the contrast between two messages: the explicit statement and the – more or less explicit – opinion.[5] Irony always contains some kind of stratification and some kind of tension between what the speaker says and what he "means" (the other opin-ions that the speaker has or might have). Examples are easy to find in everyday linguistic usage. In the wet summer of 2004, when someone standing in a light drizzle comments that it is lovely weather today, the following ambiguity may be intended:

- On the one hand the explicit – and true – communication that it is lovely weather compared with the much wetter days that have gone before;
- On the other hand the implicit – and equally true – opinion that drizzle – in contrast to what was said literally – is *not* lovely weather.

Irony can therefore consist of two sincere and conflicting messages, as in this case, but also of two insincere comments, or a sincere and an insincere communication. Irony therefore stands quite apart from truth, frankness or sincerity; it is simply a communicative technique with a tension or contrast between two different communications. In the case of the consultant who, as we have seen in Chapter 2, often practises fearless speech, however, irony generally involves two *sin-cerely held* opinions.

Other descriptions of irony are "ambiguity" or "making a subtle distinc-tion between two different parts of the same message". This subtle

---

5   Any definition of irony is open to debate, in view of the long tradition of the concept. Here I have deliberately chosen a definition in which the contrast between different communications is central. The much-used description "saying something other than what you mean" does not take account of the fact that irony also requires some transfer of "what you do mean", so that at least two things must be communicated. My definition is derived in part from Thirlwall's now classic article which coined the term "dramatic irony" (Thirlwall, 1833).

distinction may also be made non-verbally, for example by placing an exaggerated emphasis on the word "lovely" in the above example.

Because we can use irony to say more than we are literally saying or, conversely, to make clear that we know less than we are pretending to know (compare with the "sincere feigning" advocated by Kellendonk in the quotation at the start of this chapter), irony is at the same time an implicit *metacommunication*: the other person is invited to consider the (possible) messages and the contrast between them.

Two divine examples of irony

Here are two very old examples of ironic communication, followed by my interpretations.

An example: the Buddha practising irony

In sutta 5 of the Digha Nikaya, the long discourses of the Buddha (Walshe, 1987), there is a nice example of irony. A nobleman, Kutadanta, wants to hold an exceptionally grand sacrificial feast and decides to seek the advice of the Buddha, who seems to know about this sort of thing. He therefore asks the Buddha about the three-fold sacrifice and its 16 accessory instruments.

The Buddha gives him an analogy, a complicated story about another nobleman who was extremely rich and held a splendid sacrificial feast, embellished by endless associated attributes and requisites. Only in minor clauses of the story does it become clear, to the attentive listener, that the Buddha does not regard sacrifices as the most edifying activity on earth. Kutadanta realises that he cannot afford such an enormous feast and asks about sacrifices on a more modest scale. Again, the Buddha tells him about all sorts of sacrifices and why these are worth striving for. In response to Kutadanta's many questions, the Buddha gives a brief and concise answer, until Kutadanta finally realises that he is concerned with quite different, much more personal issues. At that moment, "when the Buddha knew that Kutadanta's mind was ready, pliable, free from the hindrances, joyful and calm, then he preached a sermon on Dhamma in brief: on suffering, its origin, its cessation, and the path." Everything that the Buddha had previously said about sacrifices now appears to be incomplete, indeed virtually superfluous, and therefore ironic.

An example: Apollo practising irony[6]

In the first book of his *Histories*, Herodotus tells us about Paktyes, a Greek who was appointed by the Persian king Kuros as the governor of conquered Greek territory. Paktyes rebels as soon as Kuros' back is turned, and takes back the territory.

However, with his superior power the Persian king is able to recapture the area easily, and Paktyes is forced to flee before the Persian troops. He escapes to the Greek town of Cyme, where the Persians soon arrive to demand that he be handed over. The population of Cyme is uncertain and visits a nearby oracle of Apollo to ask what they should do. The oracle says: "Hand him over to the Persians." The townspeople are about to do so when a nobleman, Aristodikos, intervenes and goes back to the oracle. He cannot believe that Apollo is asking them to hand over a supplicant. But the oracle's second answer is the same: Paktyes must be handed over to the Persians. Aristodikos, who has been expecting that answer, is still not satisfied: he walks around the temple trampling on all the birds' nests he can find. Before long a voice comes down from the innermost shrine: "Impious wretch, how dare you kill birds that come to my temple for protection?!"

Aristodikos, with a ready wit, replies: "Apollo, you protect your supplicants, but still you are instructing the people of Cyme to hand over one of their own . . .!" "Indeed", answers the god according to Herodotus, "that is what I am doing, that you may suffer the sooner for the sacrilege, and never come here again to consult my oracle about handing over supplicants."

In the above examples it is noticeable that both the Buddha and Apollo have an unambiguous message, but choose not to express it unambiguously. Both seem to wait until the nobleman in question is receptive.

They allow the receptivity to the message to develop in the other person, so to speak, from the inside. They do not remain passive until the other is receptive; on the contrary, they deliver a message that is indeed their message, but within the other's frame of reference. When the other person is the way he is (in the examples: interested in the pomp and ceremony of sacrifices to the gods or considering the option of handing over a supplicant), then a different message is appropriate, according to these two gurus.

---

6   This example is derived from Vellacott's book on irony in the tragedies of Euripides: *Ironic drama* (1975).

What the Buddha and Apollo are doing here is an extreme version of "tailoring the message to the recipient". Because they choose not to announce their divine opinion or teaching in a direct and unambiguous manner and, instead, say what they believe fits in precisely with the recipient's frame of reference, they cannot avoid communicating ironically: they do not say exactly what they are thinking in the situation in question.[7] Strikingly, both the Buddha and Apollo are able to *observe* what is going on in the minds of their interlocutors in an almost superhuman manner. If they did not have such a superbly sophisticated awareness, they would never have been able to communicate ironically. Conversely, and more generally, the reader may find that irony is just around the corner when you are observing very carefully, when you are almost "in the other person's shoes". When you say something from that other person's perspective, the message will "automatically" be ironic in many cases: the message is valid for the other person, in his frame of reference, but not necessarily in an equal manner for you as the consultant. As soon as you say something that follows naturally from what you have heard from the other person but on which you also have your own, as yet unexpressed, ideas, the communication will be ironic, as in the examples given above.

Irony redirects the focus back to what actually concerns the other person and so creates a tension between different interpretations, which is hard to shake off. That continued, tense focus easily leads to considerations "at metalevel": what else is a supplicant but a vulnerable baby bird? What precisely makes me want to sacrifice to the gods? And so on.

The ironic consultant

In which situations can irony be a useful technique for helpful outsiders? There are some circumstances which invite irony. This is particularly true when it is difficult for the other person to understand the direct message, such as:

---

7   Leaving aside the philosophical doubt as to whether anyone can ever say precisely what is going on inside oneself.

- when a price has to be paid for accepting the message: irony keeps pointing to other approaches, even when a particular path has already been embarked upon;
- inability to understand the message directly: irony affords an opportunity for a deeper, more integrated understanding (Lear, 2003);
- when the message is too painful or disappointing: irony does not raise any obstacles but in fact creates space for other ideas;
- when the message reiterates something that was rejected previously: repetition merely fosters resistance, while irony places the same message in a different perspective.

There are also circumstances in which irony in fact has certain advantages over a direct approach. These are situations where the independence or autonomy of the other person is at stake:
- When there is a possibility of (over-)dependence on the helpful outsider: irony always aims to allow the other person to make his own decision;
- When the other person finds it difficult to assume responsibility for his own situation: irony keeps the responsibility firmly with the other person;
- When a particular change is paid lip service but not actually carried out: irony can point this out by also paying lip service, but this time in an exaggerated manner;
- When a more "reflective approach" is desired; when we want to get the other person thinking: irony offers ambiguity and thus scope for reflection.

There are also circumstances in which irony seems less appropriate. Possible contra-indications:
- When the other person's sense of responsibility is extremely high: irony increases personal responsibility;
- When the other person's readiness to take action is low: irony invites further reflection, as a result of which action is further deferred;
- When the helping relationship is not yet strong enough: irony puts the relationship to the test;
- When there is a lack of trust: irony increases uncertainty.

The ironic consultant communicates ambiguously. She sends out ambiguous signals that stimulate the client to reflect.

There is another drawback to the use of irony: sarcasm and rivalry are just around the corner. It is only a small step from an ironic to a sarcastic intervention. As with the difference between fearless speech and flattery, in my view it is primarily in the *intention* that the difference between irony and sarcasm resides. Irony encourages a different way of looking at things and invites a different perspective, while sarcasm actually enforces defences as it rules out different perspectives.

How can irony be applied?
It is possible to break down ironic communication into a number of steps. All of these steps together sometimes take no more than a few seconds:
1. An impression of "incompleteness": the story told by the other person remains unfinished for the consultant. Something is missing, or the impression the consultant gets from the story is not the one the teller is describing. Think of a cheerful communication of an unpleasant story: evidently, there is something pleasant about it as well. Another example is a one-sided jubilant story that does not

quite come across. Apparently, therefore, there is something else in addition to the jubilation.

2. An impression of "difference". By dwelling on the incompleteness that strikes the consultant, he learns something about the difference between:
   - what the other person says and what he thinks and does; or
   - what he hears and what he imagines to be there as well.

   For example, we know that the person who is so enthusiastic now has done other things of which he is not at all proud. Or we know that the other person also has doubts about what has just been asserted.

3. The decision to bring up the subject of this difference. This is often necessary for the purposes of a complete summary of the received "message", which includes the ambivalence. Alternatively, the consultant as helpful outsider wants to give back or point out something that the other person does not see for himself. In many cases, it is not necessary to do this. The moment then passes, or the perceived difference moves on towards a climax.

4. The decision to bring up the subject of this difference ironically. This decision is largely intuitive and immediate. In some cases, where the other person is speaking at great length, for example, it is possible to make this decision more conscious. It may be sensible, when making this decision, to let yourself be guided by the above list of situations where irony may be useful and situations where it is better avoided. For me, another factor in the decision is the fact that the ironic intervention is fairly mild: instructing ironically or arguing ironically is almost impossible. So, if I want to try out or test something, my choice for irony will be made more quickly.

5. The ironic communication itself. It may be the emphasising of an element of the story that is apparently complete, but is not so in my view. Or the bringing up of part of "my story" – and putting it into context at the same time: "Listening to your enthusiastic story like this, I am reminded strangely of what went wrong last week. But that may have nothing to do with it?"

6. Irony often ends with a concentrated awaiting of the other person's response. This response can take a wide range of forms, from alienation to recognition, or even a surprising and often liberating discovery, the well-known expression of a genuine "learning experience" to which helpful outsiders are so attached (see Drucker, 1978).

Characteristically, irony virtually always starts with a form of irony by the other person (incompleteness, ambiguous signals, etc.), which the consultant reflects upon and makes more explicit.[8] Like all communication, irony has something two-sided and mutual about it. It is too easy to say that ironic communication lies entirely with one person. The consultant's task is often to use the implicit irony of the other person (or of the situation: see the final paragraph of this chapter) as a lever in order to introduce a new idea. This use of irony is also described by Lear (2003). Lear adds that the implicit and unconscious use of irony can be very obstructive for the client, while making it explicit, i.e. being conscious of one's own irony, almost automatically leads to a new formulation of the problem which is less ambiguous and therefore less problematic for the client.

A case study: towards a more service-oriented organisation

As a management consultant I have ample opportunity to apply irony in my own practice. An example of a situation from recent years concerns a support services department of a large university. Over a hundred people work in the department. The governing body issues the order to be more customer oriented and responsive to market forces, and cannot rule out the possibility that services will be outsourced in the future. The department is therefore in fact being threatened with closure. The recent creation of the department by an imposed merger of a number of smaller service units also indicates that the university is serious about implementing proposed changes. The new department is headed by a director who comes from the banking sector and whose behaviour shows that he is a stranger to the university's culture.

This situation leads of course to major tensions and uncertainties within the department. One thing is clear to the new director: this department needs a more service-oriented attitude. The staff needs to focus more on their customers' problems, listen better to their customers and learn to see the technical problems in which they specialise more from the viewpoint of the customer.

---

8   Jonathan Lear gives a wonderful example of irony which is actually expressed by his patient: "But how can I be angry with you – all you have done is sit here!" The patient only becomes aware of the irony when the therapist starts to examine the underlying message: "Perhaps that is precisely why you are angry" (see Lear, 2003, from page 123).

The director invites myself and some colleagues for a discussion and we orient ourselves further by talking to staff members from all levels of the organisation. Then we design a one-day programme in which, in addition to some transfer of knowledge, our main aim is to reflect on and strengthen the department's own attitude as a service provider. The management team (MT) of the organisation discusses our proposal several times. Following those discussions, we draw up a list of risks associated with the programme, which we again discuss with the MT. It is clear to us that there is a lot of anxiety and doubt within the MT concerning our programme, which we can well imagine. Focusing on service provision in this way is new for this organisation. We make attempts to discuss the doubts about the programme with the MT members, but those attempts do not go very well: it is as if we are from two different planets. In order to ensure that the programme is taken seriously across the organisation, we offer it to all of the staff and even the MT participates in a special tailor-made version.

In the MT programme it is clear from the very start that success is not on the cards today: some MT members arrive with an apparently dismissive attitude and they complain about the many regular activities that they can't afford to miss even for a day. At the end of the day they ask if this programme is the same as that for the staff, or if the programme for MT members is different. To our surprise, differences with the other version appear to be a very pertinent issue for those present. A few days later our client reports that he is very dissatisfied with the way in which we are interpreting the programme and comments in particular that it lacks any substantive transfer of knowledge in the field of service provision. The long-dormant contradictions and doubts concerning the programme come to a head. We are accused of not doing our jobs properly.

This subsequently turns out to be the turning point for this assignment, the time when we can start to become effective within the organisation. Until the special MT programme we – in the eyes of the organisation – are well-reputed consultants who will come up with an easily digestible programme on service provision. Up to that moment we have a single unambiguous message, indeed a message for which there is a need within the organisation.

Now – still in the eyes of the organisation – we are people with only a limited knowledge of service provision, consultants who are always going on about "listening better" and "flexibility" and who have to improvise to a large degree in order to maintain their own service provision. We have become consultants with a dual message, people who know less than they pretend, and who are starting to feel uncomfortable themselves.

I well remember the conversation with the client after the MT programme, especially the moment when he goes to his bookcase and takes out a book with the title *Quality of Service Provision*. He says: "That is what you should be doing, that's what the service provision programme should be focusing on." There is a dual irony here: on the part of our client, who already seems to know what we have still to teach him, the client who says "This is what you should be teaching me", and on my part: that same day I buy the book, which I had not come across before, and base a new syllabus on it, but without agreeing with the director that this is what the organisation should be learning. By taking on board the client's objections in this way, I have the opportunity to show what I understand by service provision: listening carefully and responding flexibly to clients' wishes. In later conversations with the director we occasionally return, ironically, to the new subject matter: "We have discussed the theoretical qualities of service provision again at length in the programme, and this was much appreciated. It is strange, though, that your clients show so little interest in that theory. Perhaps we should give them a course on it as well?"

Within the programme on service provision, I am therefore in agreement with my client that the programme does not connect sufficiently with what participants themselves understand by quality of service provision. Within that programme, I agree therefore that things could be improved. Outside the programme, in a broader sense, I agree that the client already knows what is meant by quality of service provision, and what good service provision is, so outside the context of the programme the client has little more to learn from the programme. Don't we all know what good service provision is, if only because we all regularly find ourselves in the role of client? But does that mean that we are always customer oriented in our daily practice? Unfortunately not. By our uncritical service attitude we show that we can agree that this organisation both knows everything there is to know about service provision *and* has a lot to learn in the field of service provision. We thereby ensure that we can continue to speak fearlessly about service provision, both within the programme and in our relationship with the client.

The programme as a whole has since been completed for all of the staff, with evaluations which are, to be quite honest, very positive. Moreover, we are pleased to hear from our contacts that the staff of the support services department have become more customer oriented.

Irony as an instrument for change

Irony generates movement from the inside

In most treatises on communication (see, for example, Schulz von Thun, 1982, DeVito, 1985, or Hargie, 1986), irony is either not mentioned at all or portrayed as something comparable to swearing in church: irony and ambiguous communication are either not talked about or used in examples of "bad" communication.[9] In such instructive texts about "effective communication" we learn that the message in communication must be clear and, above all, unambiguous. We learn how to put into words clearly and honestly what is going on in ourselves at many communicative levels and how to ensure that the signals at the different levels are congruent (such as content, procedure, interaction, emotion – see also Chapter 2 of De Haan & Burger, 2004), and so to communicate as clearly, purely and unambiguously as possible.

Nevertheless, irony is often an appropriate form of communication in a changing situation. Change, like irony, is characterised by a tension between the old and the new. This tension is often a driving force behind the success of outsiders in change: outsiders make the contrast between "old" and "new", between "unsatisfactory" and "worth pursuing" explicit, by being present in the situation as a significant third party.

It seems worthwhile to honour both different – and conflicting – aspects of change in communication at the same time, and that is very possible through the use of irony. Consider a person who is talking light-heartedly about personal changes awaiting him. We might say: "Some people would have a lot of trouble really taking that step, but that is obviously not the case for you." Or someone who we think is overdramatising the imminent changes. We can go along with his overdramatisation, or even take it further, but in an ironic tone: "Goodness, those are really daunting changes for you; quite terrifying, aren't they?"

Irony often has an "unfreezing" effect and invites movement – movement from one perspective to another. The direction of the technique is often from pushing to pulling on the one hand and, on the other hand, from action to reflection (so from skills to the underlying inten-

---

9   An interesting exception is the book *Equivocal communication* (Bavelas *et al.*, 1990), which makes careful study of the power and properties of ambiguous communication.

tion). In the first place the familiar *locus of evaluation* (see Rogers, 1951), or the focus of self-assessment, is shifted from the consultant to the person who is undergoing the change. Irony sometimes comprises a judgement, but at the same time an alternative to it, so that the decision is left to the recipient. This illustrates the movement of irony: the consultant's opinion is present, but at the same time nuanced by a second opinion.

Because the movement takes place from the inside, there is less chance of resistance. After all, there is no unambiguous communication which the other person can oppose. There is only the contrast between different points of view or options. It is precisely in this contrast that the greatest effectiveness of irony lies: the consultant builds up and maintains a tension between the different options. Not all of the options are explicit and some are consequently not easy to rule out. The only thing that is clear is that intriguing alternatives are possible for the self-chosen option . . .

Irony can be applied both directively and non-directively
A distinction is often made between directive and non-directive techniques with regard to instruments for change, i.e. between pushing and pulling (see De Haan & Burger, 2004). Extreme examples in the psychotherapy literature are Carl Rogers (1951), as a great advocate of the non-directive method, and Milton Erickson, as a master of the – often brief and intensive – directive method (see, for example, Rosen, 1982).

Irony can be applied both directively and non-directively and acts like a bridge between the extreme directive and non-directive methods, because – like both of the latter – it works largely from the basis of the internal frame of reference of the person undergoing the change. The two "divine" examples above also illustrate how Apollo applies irony directively (pushing, leading), while the Buddha adopts a non-directive (pulling, reflecting) approach.

The points of contact between irony and both directive and non-directive techniques start at the place where opinion-forming or evaluation is centred (Rogers' *locus of evaluation*). It is shifted *within the person undergoing the change* and remains there. If we stay truly close to the other person's frame of reference, irony is often unavoidable in our communicative actions. In this connection Rogers introduced[10] the terms *unconditional positive regard* and *acceptance*, which emphasise the concentration on and acceptance of the other person's frame of reference, and *congruence* and *transparence*, which emphasise recognition and acceptance of the consultant's own frame of reference. He therefore asks helpful outsiders to penetrate deeply into both frames of reference *at the same time*. Because these two frames of reference differ, a contrast between two realities develops automatically, and if this contrast becomes part of the communication, the communication is automatically ironic. Affectionate irony can clearly be seen in film excerpts of Rogers working with clients.

On the other hand, the practice of irony with a contrast that is so extreme that the different messages exclude each other, in combination with directivity, leads to what is known as the *paradoxical injunction* (Watzlawick *et al.*, 1967). This is a well-known directive technique which was developed at Stanford University, partly on the basis of a study of Erickson's directive methods. Both messages in the paradox are derived from messages from the other person to the helping outsider. The classic example is the client's "change paradox": "Help me without changing me", in which the client seeks and excludes change at the same time, to which the psychotherapist responds "Don't change, but be your spontaneous self" – a new paradox, which asks the other person to be spontaneous yet at the same time follow the consultant's instructions (see also Watzlawick *et al.*, 1967).

However, the essence of the effect of the paradox in the above-mentioned directive literature is that the paradox remains a riddle and cannot be solved by the other person. The paradox itself must remain implicit, so that it can operate as a *double bind*,[11] which preserves the change (Watzlawick *et al.*, 1967).

---

10 Definitions can be found in Rogers (1961). *Acceptance* is a warm recognition of the other person as a person with inherent value; *unconditional positive regard* is a noticeably positive feeling towards the other person, without reserve or evaluation. *Congruence* means agreement between the way we come across and the way we are inside – in other words, little contrast between what we say and what we think! – and *transparence* means being open to feelings and ideas that we have at this moment.

11 The *double bind* arises, according to Watzlawick *et al.* (1967), as a consequence of the paradoxical injunction, because the other person cannot escape the injunction either by carrying it out or by not carrying it out. In both cases, he is under the influence of the person giving the injunction. The injunction therefore places the other person under a double bind.

In irony, a more general technique that only requires contrast and not a mutually exclusive antithesis, this effect is only temporary: the other person usually sees through the irony at the same time that insight dawns or the change takes place, as demonstrated by the "divine" examples given above.

In irony, too, the consultant communicates largely implicitly, but that need not necessarily remain so: Apollo's intervention derives its power from the making explicit of the irony! Even if the irony is directive, the consultant nevertheless, through the dual communication, leaves the burden of final decision and responsibility to the person undergoing the change.

An example[12]

If consultants are able to detect the irony in a presenting problem, they may often save themselves a lot of work. We discovered this a little late, some 10 years ago, when we were asked to facilitate a programme on project management for Nike Europe in Belgium. Over the previous years, the Nike managers concerned had made a considerable effort towards becoming professional project leaders, reading books and attending other courses, but for some reason this had never brought them the hoped-for improvement in their work. After some preliminary conversation and agreement on the programme design, we started to facilitate the first module. The managers responded enthusiastically, inquiring about ways to complete projects more successfully. When it came to the writing of a project plan and the need to map project goals, results and milestones, someone gave a different and unexpected response: "This won't work over here. We always follow our company motto *Just do it!*, which inspires us to believe that nothing is impossible so long as we dedicate ourselves to it one hundred percent. So it won't suit us to create a lot of paperwork first and only then to begin to actually do things." This was such a compelling remark that we decided to use the remainder of the module to discuss the intentions of the participants and the circumstances under which they might be prepared to commit to any planning ahead and thereby to complement their motto. We decided to cancel the second module because we were convinced that there was no lack of knowledge or training in the field of project management. The strong company culture and motto of Nike had led to repeated ironical requests for training in the field of project management. As far as I know, this might still be the case . . .

12 I have obtained permission from Nike to publish this example which could not be presented in a more anonymous way.

Irony and the concept of fate

Ironic messages are often vague or ambiguous and make the recipient think. For this reason, irony has been compared with other uncertainties in our existence that make us think, such as "the meaning of life" or "fate". Sometimes, a distinction is made between *verbal irony* and *situational irony*, of which only the former has been discussed here so far. Situational irony is not communicated, but is experienced in the course of one's life. Consider the example of Maria Montessori. She introduced a teaching method that gives children more space, but she herself had to hide away her illegitimate son due to the moral standards of the time. This is a well-known and seemingly rare example. In my experience, however, it is possible to find situational irony all around us with a bit of practice.[13] I myself experience situational irony in relation to the subject of irony itself: I enjoy irony and find it all around me, but rarely manage to talk about it in other than unambiguous terms. Ironic consulting therefore remains a sort of unachievable and elusive state for me, which becomes all the more desirable the less achievable it is. Other examples can be found every day in the world of politics, for example when we notice world leaders being increasingly confronted with the very things they are so keen to exterminate.

Irony is embraced by the followers of a philosophy in which different incommensurable or irreconcilable realities exist side by side, which are "equally true and untrue". They use irony to tempt their readers themselves to think again about philosophical issues.[14] Plato, the ironi-

---

13 I assume that the disproportionate amount of situational irony in our lives originates in the ubiquitous defence of *sublimation* (Freud, 1936), which attempts to overcome a deep-seated internal problem by diverting energy away from it, towards constructive work. That constructive work will show traces of its origin, for example by being devoted to other people with the same problem or to some generalised aspect of the same problem. Like all defences, sublimation must constantly be "kept going". Inevitably, therefore, the defence occasionally breaks down. At those times the person with the "sublimation defence" finds himself again in the thrall of his underlying problem, apparently coincidentally stumbling upon precisely the thing he was working himself away from. An interesting example of situational irony can be found in the career choice of a consultant, when that originates from the so-called *helper's syndrome*, in which case situational irony may expose the intrinsic need of the helpful outsider for help. This syndrome is discussed in greater depth in Chapter 10.

14 See, for example, Plato (4th century BC), whose work is crammed with irony, Kierkegaard (1841), who devoted a PhD thesis to Plato's socratic irony, and postmodern authors such as Rorty (1989) or Hutcheon (1995).

cus *par excellence*, is brave enough, for example, to knock down his doctrine of Ideas completely in the *Parmenides* (fourth century BC). Because he has his character Parmenides do this with an extremely boring argument and a meaningless conclusion,[15] the reader automatically feels invited to reconsider the existence of Ideas nevertheless.

Since people who are experiencing change often ask unanswerable questions in this connection ("What will the future bring?", "What is my fate?", "Why did this have to happen to me?"), it is useful to examine the parallels between irony and the concept of fate in greater depth.

In situational irony, the role of the ironic, helpful outsider is assumed by the abstraction "fate", a sort of omniscient director of our lives. This ironic director (see also Thirlwall, 1833) teaches us modesty, by showing us that:
- our greatest strength is also our greatest weakness;
- the things that we previously yearned for and now own appear to be worth much less than we thought before we had them;
- what we wish for actually happens, sometimes to our surprise and disappointment;
- the danger in our lives is often concealed by and even caused by our false sense of security.

This irony of fate develops spontaneously, while we are changing: earlier ambitions seem less important, our strengths turn out to be weaknesses and we start to value those things that we had previously thought unimportant. You might wonder whether the concept of fate is necessary for these ironic experiences, just as it remains the question whether the helpful outsider is necessary for the experience of "irony" in change!

I will return to situational irony in Chapter 10.

---

15 "Whether one is or is not, it and the others both are and are not, and both appear and do not appear all things in all ways, both in relation to themselves and in relation to each other" (*Parmenides*, 166C). My interpretation of the ending as meaningless is not universally shared by all experts: in the face of irony ultimately one cannot know which interpretation is (most) intended unless the author is still alive so that we can ask.

Conclusion

In this chapter I wanted to stand up for ironic communication, which is often portrayed in an unfavourable light as "speaking ambiguously", or dragged by the post-modernists from a favourable light into the dark of obscure language (de-)constructions, and then used as an intentional alienation strategy (see, for example, Rorty, 1989). I hope that I have shown here that irony can preserve the proximity of different points of view, and that irony can help to bring about a movement that has a sound grounding within the person who has a need for change and movement.

We can imagine irony at the middle of a sliding scale with "congruence" and "sarcasm" at either end. Congruent communication means only reacting to the overt behaviour or words of the other person, and sarcasm means bringing out the other person's more hidden signals to such an extent that one disqualifies the overt behaviour. The consultant attempts to achieve mastery by staying away from these extremes and feeling comfortable in the middle zone, applying irony in a variety of situations.

Summary: problem formulation and irony

Verbal irony is a way of communicating that is characterised by **contrast** between two simultaneous messages: the explicit statement and the – more or less explicit – opinion.

This **contrast** – or **ambivalence** – is often already present in the client's problem:
- Contrast between the situation now and the desired situation;
- Contrast between what has to change and what has to remain stable;
- Contrast between the current approach/method and the justification of that approach/method;
- Contrast between the request for a consultant and the need to remain autonomous.

These forms of ambivalence are often **implicit** and unconscious on the part of the client. The consultant as listener can bring out and make explicit one of these ambivalences, so introducing irony.

The **effect** of ironic communication is to encourage movement from the inside by maintaining the tension and proximity between the ambivalent issues.

An **intervention schedule** that makes use of irony:
1. An impression of incompleteness: there seems to be something missing in the client's story . . .
2. An impression of difference: there seems to be a contrast between what the other person says and what he does, or feels, or leaves out . . .
3. A need to work with this difference: the consultant decides to go ahead . . .
4. A need to bring up the whole difference, so as to convey a double message . . .
5. The ironic communication itself . . .
6. Waiting and listening for the client's response . . .

In **situational irony** the circumstances take over the consultant's role, in a way. We discover that our situation is of an ironic nature, our greatest strength turns out to be our greatest weakness, the certainties in our lives turn out to be illusory, etc. Situational irony can also be made explicit in consulting processes.

5
Characteristics of Intervening

In the phase following the exploration, the consultant becomes most aware of his own contribution. The aim of consulting seems now *to make the impact of the consulting relationship visible*. It is entirely natural for a consultant, after the initial contact and exploration of the problem, to experience increasing pressure to assume a more central and self-confident role. It may be that the consultant feels a need to intervene, or the client may be watching the consultant more carefully, asking himself what the consultant is thinking and what he sees as the next step.

The client's expectation – or, in some cases, hope and fantasy – is often that the consultant will now really make a difference, that he will start to make suggestions or start to solve problems. However, in the case of real and persisting problems which have evolved over time and become an established part of the client's routines, making a difference is rarely straightforward or simple. Without much difficulty and often without even intending to, the client can distort or displace interventions by the consultant and so minimise their impact. Sometimes it is as if we are at the theatre and have been naive enough to intervene in the play, perhaps by shouting something to the actors. All around us, people are hissing, the actors are trying to ignore us as far as possible and are concentrating as best they can on the scenario that they play out every evening.

Obvious interventions often have the effect of exacerbating problems instead of alleviating them. The consultant who is conscious of his own limitations as an outsider and of the great capacity of clients to render interventions harmless will start to think differently about "making a difference". This consultant knows that it may be worthwhile to start by making a difference in the relationship with the client, by adopting a different position within the relationship. For this reason, this is often the phase in which the client/consultant relationship is tested most, either by conventional interventions that do not make a difference, or by more daring, relationship-changing interventions that do.

Most consultants will now take a look, together with the client, at the information and ideas that they gathered in the previous phase. They give feedback or say something about their own impressions and experiences during the information-gathering process. In so doing, they become more conscious of their own presence and of the possible impact that their presence may have. They are also more conscious of their own opinions and emotions. Consultants must therefore ask themselves carefully, on a regular basis, which opinions and emotions originate within themselves, and which in their client or the client's situation. Only then can they intervene in a manner that is appropriate to the client's problem and the client's situation, and derives as little as possible from their own idiosyncrasies, experiences and preconceptions. In short, the question asked by the consultant boils down to: "What belongs to whom?" or "What is going on? For whom?"

Self-monitoring: the consultant records a film of herself during the consulting conversation. She watches herself closely and considers alternative interventions.

As a thought experiment, to make myself more conscious of my own opinions and emotions and of their origins, I often imagine that I am "stepping outside myself" and recording a film of the situation, with the client and myself as their consultant. I imagine that I am looking from the outside at my situation with the client – including myself as part of that situation and even including myself as observer of that situation[1] – and I attempt to use that "film" to inform my own actions. In short, I try to engage in *self-monitoring* and *self-directing*. I use myself as an instrument to find out what belongs to the client and what to myself, and to predict how various reactions or interventions may work out in this situation. I therefore attempt to observe myself in the interaction with my client (self-monitoring), to develop a range of possible approaches and to adapt my approach flexibly (self-direction). As a result I notice that, as a consultant, I *choose* a particular intervention more consciously, note the effects of my interventions and respond to those effects with more and different interventions.

However, the quality of this "self-monitoring" is always relative, because we cannot really step outside ourselves. We can only strive for a perspective that is as independent as possible. Self-monitoring is an *interpreting* activity. It is exposed to what is known as the "hermeneutic circle" (Schleiermacher, 1805–1833), which states that your interpretations are always bound by earlier interpretations and so you rarely or never discover anything new.

Arjo Nijk (1978) has applied the hermeneutic circle to the practice of the helpful outsider. During consulting, according to Nijk, the client attempts to use stories to break through a deadlock in his own actions and to change over to new actions. Hermeneutics shows that all sorts of interpretative circles arise here (Nijk, 1978):
1. The client tries to interpret himself and his issue while relating to and engaging with the consultant.
2. The client tries to interpret his own stories, while he is telling them, in pursuit of new meanings and nuances.

---

1   The way I conduct this self-examination is also relevant to my contribution as consultant: what biases do I bring, what point of view do I adopt and what automatic preconceptions do I assume? Schön (1983) writes about this extensively and cites reflection-in-action and reflection-on-reflection-in-action as essential qualities of the consulting professional.

3. The client tries to interpret the consultant's words and actions, in order to fit them into his own stories and actions.
4. The consultant tries at the same time to understand and interpret the client's stories and actions – and thereby also to interpret the problem and the client's situation in turn.
5. The consultant tries to interpret his own contribution to the client's stories and his own responses to them.
6. The consultant tries to understand and interpret himself as a consultant.

These are cyclical processes, because each party in the consulting conversation advances from an existing interpretation, via new facts and new words, to a new interpretation, and so on. In this interpretative process there is no understanding without pre-understanding, no knowledge without pre-knowledge and no judgement without prejudice. Every new fact or word is only a minor modification, a tiny ripple in the stream of existing interpretations. Consultant and client are therefore both entangled in a web of interpretations. Indeed, some philosophers are so pessimistic as to claim that new understanding *is fundamentally* impossible, because you can never free yourself of existing understanding and the existing conversation. Whatever the case, it is worthwhile being conscious of these hermeneutic circles when participating as objectively and critically as possible in self-monitoring, in order to gather information for alternative interpretations and interventions.

In this phase, more than in any other, the consultant is confronted with his own *choice of role* with respect to the client and client issue, i.e. with his own *contribution* to the client's situation. Because intervening always takes place with a view to learning or changing the client or situation, possible role interpretations depend, in my view, on the type of learning or changing envisaged. In order to make a clear distinction between different roles, it is worthwhile looking at the type of learning that can be facilitated by consultants. This examination is based on a widely accepted, general framework for different forms of learning, David Kolb's experiential learning model (1984; see also De Haan, 2004b). This model distinguishes four learning styles, which correspond to four consulting roles (see the figure below):

1. The facilitator of *assimilative learning* or learning by translating observations and reflections into concepts and models, is the *expert*, the consultant who focuses primarily on knowledge and solutions.
2. The facilitator of *convergent learning* or learning by translating concepts and models into hypotheses or solutions, is the *process manager*, the consultant who focuses primarily on relatedness and progress.
3. The facilitator of *accommodative learning* or learning by trying out solutions and actively experimenting, is the *developer*, the consultant who focuses primarily on new approaches and feedback.
4. The facilitator of *divergent learning* or learning by looking at specific situations from different perspectives, is the *coach*, the consultant who focuses primarily on new perspectives and questions.

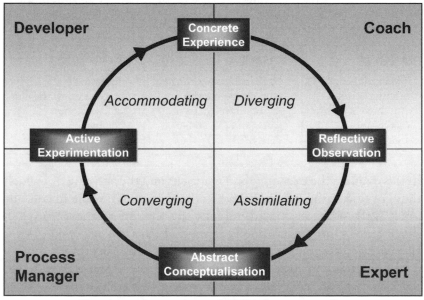

Four consulting roles and Kolb's learning cycle.

There are two other well-known proposals for possible role choices in the literature, namely those of Tilles[2] (1961) and Block (1981). Tilles (1961) distinguishes:

2 This model has become widely known mainly as a result of a later adaptation by Schein (1969).

1. the *purchase/sale model*: contributing the right information or the "right answer";
2. the *doctor/patient model*: prescribing the right medicine or solutions; and
3. the *constructive process model*: jointly undertaking a process in the direction of improvement.

Tilles writes primarily about expert advice; only in the constructive process model does the client himself become part of the consulting. This *process consultant* therefore has characteristics of all three of the other roles: process manager, developer and coach.

Block (1981) sets his sights wider than simply consulting: he proposes roles which overlap with other common activities within work organisations:

Managing	Consulting	Executing
"Monitoring and directing activities with the aim of a successful completion"	"Collaborating with the aim of bringing about an improvement in the situation of the other person"[3]	"Carrying out activities with the aim of a successful completion"

In this diagram the executers and managers and the activities for which they are responsible are *themselves* in the foreground, while in consulting it is the *other person* and his activities that are in the foreground. Block (1981) introduces the (1) *expert*, (2) *"pair of hands"* and (3) *collaborative* roles – the "pair of hands" is in fact an executing and not a consulting role, the expert corresponds to my definition of expert, and the collaborative role, like Tilles' *process manager*, fulfils a sort of transcendent consulting role which has features of the roles of process manager, developer and coach. Other descriptions of consultants' roles, such as those in Kubr (1996), adopt the spectrum from directive to non-directive interventions (see Chapter 4) as the decisive criterion.

My roles also show some overlap with the other activities within organisations, as the following diagram illustrates:

---

3   According to my definition in the prologue to this book.

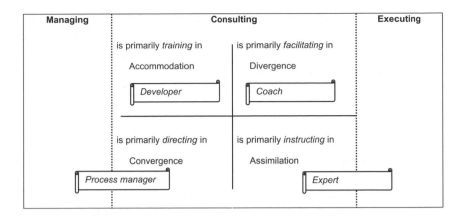

The process manager will therefore sometimes take the lead in projects and the expert will sometimes take on part of the execution. This applies even more strongly the other way round: the manager must be a process manager and the executing "pair of hands" an expert. Only the developer and the coach turn out, in most circumstances, to be "pure" consulting roles.

The preferred learning styles of the consultant do not always correspond to the role that he usually adopts. It is precisely because consulting aims to facilitate the other person's learning[4] that the consultant often prefers to learn in a divergent learning style, which may be different from the style preferred by the client. Nevertheless, it often helps for a coach to be coached himself or for an expert to have learned a lot in the field of his own expertise. However, most consultants know many examples of situations in which they, as the client, behaved entirely differently from the way in which they recommend their own clients to behave. Time and again, it turns out darkest directly beneath the lighthouse! The following chapter revisits my four consulting roles from the perspective of the art of intervening.

Some consultants, especially the coaches, choose not to intervene explicitly, even in this phase. They invite the client just to explore and consider the situation with them and facilitate the client's quest for possible solutions. Other consultants intervene so strongly that they influence the relationship with the client. In any case, a good

---

4 A definition which I will explain in more detail in Chapter 7.

consultant notes and manages his own contribution. In order to with-stand the tensions which may arise in this phase in particular, a good relationship between client and consultant *and* agreement on that relationship are extremely important.

In most cases the client now feels invited to look at his own situation differently or even to start changing it. The consultant actually inter-venes in the situation, so that this is the main phase where *resistance to change* may emerge. Resistance manifests itself in a variety of ways, ranging from open revolt to, ironically enough, strong support for the new proposals. Powerful emotions often come into play. The aim is to let go of old patterns, while the new patterns intended to replace them have not yet been tried out. This often results in extreme uncertainty and anxiety, which express themselves as resistance. The art is to find one's way to the next phase, in which the change takes place from the inside and is therefore self-maintaining.

It is interesting to investigate the exact source of resistance. At the start, the client often asks what or who is to blame for the undesirable situation. The consultant will attempt to convert the question of blame, which is unproductive, into a question of responsibilities. In addition, instead of looking backwards, the consultant will often want to consider future responsibilities and the divisions of responsibilities that will lead to the required improvements. If the consultant emphati-cally and forcefully defends his proposals for the future, it is possible that he will come into opposition to the client and resistance will result. As a result, any resistance is by no means all down to the client: the consultant is also partly responsible. Resistance often arises because the consultant takes on too much responsibility for the situation. A considered, original, apposite opinion in this phase can be enough to set a change in motion: once the client has a different perception of the situation, he will then be the main specialist in the field of solu-tions (Block, 1981).

In the following chapter I want to look at exactly what happens when the consultant intervenes, and at different forms of intervention. I devote particular attention to politics and power in organisations, to which the consultant is increasingly exposed at this stage of the process or when intervening more actively – and in which he must therefore increasingly participate.

♬

Summary: characteristics of intervening

Consulting is a temporary collaborative relationship between client and consultant, the objective of which is an improvement in the client's fortunes.

Consulting is also an attitude or state of mind on the part of the consultant, which takes the following forms:
1. **Fearless speech**: open and honest, without fear of the consequences;
2. **Exploration**: listening to and interpreting whatever the client brings;
3. **Self-monitoring and self-direction**: the ability to examine and guide consulting itself from a different, sometimes more objective, perspective;
4. **Facilitating change**: being present during change, respecting the autonomous nature of change;
5. **Letting go** of the client and the client's situation, practising detachment *vis-à-vis* the change that, as a consultant, one has become personally involved in.

In the third phase, that of **intervening in the client's situation**, the art of consulting appears to consist primarily in the application of **self-monitoring** and **self-directing**, in order to find a path through resistance towards a situation in which the change is self-maintaining.

Different consultants **intervene** in different ways:
1. The **expert** contributes knowledge and knowledge-based solutions.
2. The **process manager** contributes relatedness and progress.
3. The **developer** suggests new approaches and influences by means of feedback.
4. The **coach** opens up new perspectives and asks penetrating questions.

Intervening is **helping to get change off the ground**. Because consulting develops in the consulting relationship, this change may also relate to the role adopted by the consultant and to the consulting relationship itself.

As a result, intervening often puts pressure on the existing situation and the existing relationship. The art is to avoid unnecessary **resistance** in that respect.

6
Intervening and Power

Nor do I see any way of avoiding either the infamy or the danger other than by putting the case with moderation instead of assuming responsibility for it, and by stating one's views dispassionately and defending them alike dispassionately and modestly; so that, if the city or the leader accepts your advice, he does so of his own accord, and will not seem to have been driven to it by your importunity.

(Machiavelli, *Discorsi*, circa 1519)

Intervening means stepping in

In developing a response to a request for advice, the consultant always has to "step in". The Latin word *intervenire* means literally coming between, or stepping in, mediating, exerting influence, and even interfering and disrupting.

It is artificial to refer to a "moment" or a "phase" in which the consultant begins to "disrupt" or step in. Right from the first contact, the consultant is already stepping in to some degree of course, because it is then that he is making an initial connection with the client. But it is often not until much later that the "stepping in" becomes central, when the consultant expresses an opinion or proposes a course of action, for example. It is not always clear "who is intervening in whose situation": the client also triggers things in the consultant, by way of recognition and involvement, for example.

The motion of stepping in is highly significant for consultants, because it opens a communicative *triangle*, in which the consultant forms the third angle. We can therefore imagine the client at one end of a line with his issue at the other end, turned to face the issue, often "opposing" the issue in some way (see figure on page 65). The consultant ideally adopts a "third", independent position and identifies neither with the issue nor with the client. The situation after the consultant's entry therefore resembles a triangle with connections between each pair of vertices. This is a shifting of attention from two to three: whatever the consultant does – and even if he does nothing – a huge change has already taken place! This triangle perfectly illustrates the fact that the consultant has now become part of a system. The triangle has made an entrance at various locations in the literature on consulting, a small selection of which is given here:

1 the basic intervention triangle
The consultant steps in between client and issue in some way. He can do so in a number of ways: the consultant can say something about the way in which he relates to the problem himself, about different postures or attitudes of the client and about different aspects of the problem. The consultant can therefore place the emphasis more or less on the client and more or less on the problem, and can say more or less about the third angle: himself.
(this triangle has been introduced along with structural family therapy by Minuchin, 1974, and was adapted to a coaching context by O'Neill, 2000)

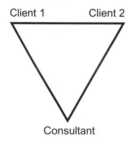

2 the mediation triangle
The consultant intervenes in the client organisation in some way and says something about the way in which different clients or client systems relate to each other. This intervention model is found in management consulting, conflict mediation and arbitration.
(see, for example, Van Dongen, *et al.*, 1996)

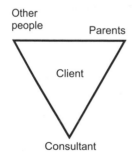

3 the transference triangle
This triangle is often a consequence of the first two. The consultant is now part of a client triangle, where the client repeats patterns that he has "practised" with important figures in his life: parents or significant others, such as immediate colleagues at work – and now the consultant. The transference triangle comes from psychoanalytical therapy and is a good way of illustrating how the consultant becomes "part of the system" while intervening.
(see Malan, 1995)

There are also triangles that the client has already created and of which the consultant will form part as a result of intervening:

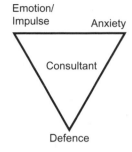

Emotion/
Impulse　　　　Anxiety

Consultant

Defence

4 the conflict triangle

This triangle, like the previous one, comes from the world of psychoanalysis and is very useful in consulting and coaching. The client has a particular need, a particular emotion or a particular *impulse*, the presence or potential realisation of which creates *anxieties*. As a result, he uses a *defence* (see Freud, 1936) to banish those unpleasant anxieties or to avoid acting on the impulse. Only the consequences of the defence are visible – the rest of the triangle is "under the surface" of the client's behaviour.[1] It is worthwhile for consultants, via the partly visible defence, to make contact with the underlying anxieties and hidden emotions or impulses. This often leads to a deepening of the relationship between consultant and client, and to more insight into the client's problem.
(see Malan, 1995)

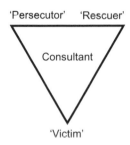

'Persecutor'　　'Rescuer'

Consultant

'Victim'

5 the drama triangle

(also known as the *rescuer's triangle* or *Karpman triangle*)
The drama triangle is an example of the transference triangle in a form which occurs relatively frequently.[2] Here, the transference is between two corners of the triangle, where the client enters into a game of rescuer/victim, persecutor/victim or persecutor/rescuer. It is a macabre game in which ordinary "giving" and "taking" are distorted

---

1　In the long term, nested triangles can occur here. With repeated use, a defence can become a habit, which itself creates new anxieties in turn. New defences can be set up in turn against these new anxieties. To my knowledge, these secondary anxieties and defences were first described by Isabel Menzies (1960), at an organisational level.
The Epilogue contains a detailed consulting example in which secondary anxieties play a role. This example concerns secondary anxieties that are posing an obstacle in a professional setting but appear to be closely connected with primary anxieties in original family relationships.

2　Clearly, the drama triangle is only one of many triangular dramatic situations that a consultant could become exposed to. To prepare oneself for a variety of dramatic situations it can be very helpful to either experience dramatic performances or read summaries of archetypal dramatic situations. A classic in the latter field is *The thirty-six dramatic situations* by Georges Polti (1895), where triangles abound. What makes Polti's book especially worthwhile is the fact that he has painstakingly reviewed hundreds of plays of world drama and determined to which of the 36 dramatic situations each of them belongs. Karpman's drama triangle is the same as the second dramatic triangle in Polti's book, and Polti gives as examples *Don Quixote* (as a parody) and *Lohengrin*, among others.

into blaming and complaining exchanges. What is special about the drama triangle in practice is the fact that the client keeps jumping to a different corner when things get too hot for him in one corner.

There is a huge temptation for the consultant to step into the drama triangle himself, via the role left open by the client. Very often in consulting, this is the role of "rescuer", although it can also happen via one of the other two corners. At that moment he starts to play a role in the repetition, and *not* in the solution, of the same game. The client then oscillates between the corners of the triangle, doomed to keep repeating the same motion. He starts, for example, as a person seeking help as a "victim", but as soon as the consultant responds with assistance, the client moves to "persecutor" and responds critically. If the consultant has tried this a couple of times and seems despondent, the client acts as "rescuer" and cheers the consultant up. (see Karpman, 1968)

The art for the consultant is often to enter into the interaction with the triangle, but at the same time to remain independent:
1. In the *intervention triangle* there is a risk of *taking over* the client's problem.
2. In the *mediation triangle* there is a risk of *becoming directly involved* in the conflict in the client organisation.
3. In the *transference triangle* there is a risk of *countertransference* without recognising the client's transference (also known as *projective identification* – see, for example, Czander, 1993).
4. In the *conflict triangle* there is a risk of *exposing* too much, as a result of which the increasing anxiety only reinforces the defence (see Malan, 1995).
5. In the *drama triangle* there is a risk, as mentioned above, of *becoming part* of the client's repetitive games.

In fact, from the perspective of most of these triangles, we encounter the same risk again and again: becoming too closely and inappropriately involved and thereby losing control of one's own interaction with the client. Only in the conflict triangle is the risk precisely the opposite: here, the consultant can break through the client's control to such an extent that the client or client organisation gets a feeling of losing control.

The focus of interventions

Let us look at the basic intervention triangle again, this time more closely. If we enlarge this triangle further, we find different aspects of client and problem on which the consultant can focus to a greater or lesser degree with his interventions (see figure below).

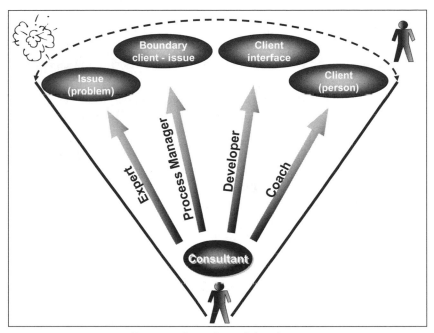

Four consulting roles and their focus.

Depending on the emphasis which the consultant, together with the client, places in the intervention, there are a number of different *role choices* for the consultant:

1. (*Focused on the problem*) Some consultants intervene strongly in relation to the problem, for example by contributing solutions or redefining the problem. These consultants are known as experts or *expert consultants*. They intervene from a basis of particular knowledge of or experience with problems of this sort. In extreme cases they work on the problem without any involvement of the client and then later "deliver" the "solved" problem to the client, as it were. In these cases the triangle almost disappears and degenerates into the consultant/problem line, which takes the place of the

client/problem line. Examples are scientists, teachers and other experts.

2. (*Focused on the connection between client and problem*) Some consultants intervene strongly in the relationship between client and problem, for example by examining the involvement of the client and other parties, the progress made, the approaches taken in the past or the "management" of the problem. I call these consultants *process managers*. They examine the problem together with the client and help with managing the problem and involving other parties. The mediation triangle is most applicable to these consultants. Examples are project managers, interim managers and mediators.

3. (*Focused on the behaviour and approach of the client*) Some consultants intervene strongly on the activities and behaviours of the client and try to bring about improvements in this respect. I call these consultants (management) *developers*. They often consider alternative behaviours and help the client to experiment with new behaviour. Trainers and facilitators of change processes often adopt this role. Other examples are (driving) instructors, role-play actors and sports coaches.

4. (*Focused on the perspectives and preconceptions of the client*) Some consultants intervene strongly on the personal development of the client and attempt, together with the client, to consider alternative assumptions, perspectives and starting points. We call these *coaches*. They often consider patterns that are visible in the behaviour or attitude of the client but of which the client is unaware. In extreme cases they work exclusively with the client's untapped potential, without looking directly at (solutions to) the problem. They then "deliver" a "rejuvenated" client who starts to examine and approach his own problems in a new way. In these cases the triangle almost disappears and degenerates into the client/consultant line, which therefore takes the place of the client/problem line. Examples are therapists, organisation developers and executive coaches.

As already demonstrated in Chapter 5, these four roles correspond to the four different forms of experiential learning differentiated by Kolb (1984). Each of these consulting roles focuses on a different learning style (see also Chapter 16 of De Haan, 2004b, and Appendix B at the end of this book).

It may help to look at slightly exaggerated "parodies" of the four consulting roles:[3]

1. The expert who has become a caricature of himself handles client and problem like a *Mr Fix-It*: "Give me your problem, I'll solve it for you and it'll be ready tomorrow."

2. The process consultant who becomes a caricature of himself handles client and problem like an international *peace broker*, constantly taking soundings and coordinating behind the scenes, thereby maintaining a tenuous connection between parties who want little to do with each other. "Let's try again to get everyone together and force a breakthrough."

3. The developer who has become a caricature of himself degenerates into the *animal trainer* of his clients, endlessly teaching them new tricks and coping mechanisms without ever tackling the underlying problem or the underlying abilities or inabilities of the client. "If you really believe it, you can do it."

4. The coach who becomes a caricature of himself handles client and problem like a *psychoanalyst*, endlessly generating new interpretations and insights without worrying too much about their practical implementation, or about decision-making and solutions. "What is a person like you doing with a problem like this?"

---

3 Interestingly, Plutarch (109, 59F) too gives a number of more negative parodies of the four consulting roles, in the form of consultants who have become caricatures of themselves and been tempted into flattering behaviour:

1. (expert) "A flatterer, typically, has nothing to say about the actual speech of a ludicrously awful orator, but criticizes the sound of his voice and takes him to task for ruining his throat by drinking cold water; or if he is told to go through an atrocious script, he criticizes the roughness of the papyrus and the careless untidiness of the writer."

2. (process manager) "He energetically and forcefuly lambasts the culprit if he sees a tool out of place, a case of poor housekeeping, or someone not bothering to have a haircut or dressing carelessly or paying inadequate attention to a dog or a horse. He is totally unconcerned, however, if someone neglects his parents, ignores his children, humiliates his wife, sneers at his relatives and ruins his assets; these situations find him tongue-tied and helpless."

3. (developer) "Or the flatterer is like a schoolteacher who scolds his pupil for his writing tablet and writing instrument, while ignoring his flawed and faulty language."

4. (coach) "He is like a coach who lets an athlete get drunk and live an undisciplined life, and then makes an issue of the poor quality of the oil bottle and scraper used for anointing the body."

Role choice: the consultant can focus on four different aspects during a consulting conversation: the person of the client, the client's behaviour, the interface between client and problem and the problem itself.

In most consulting assignments the choice of role will not be so extreme and the consultant will opt for a combination of interventions from different roles. It is interesting to consider for yourself what sort of interventions and which consulting roles you have tended to adopt in your own consulting practice. We have developed an instrument for assessing the nature of the consultant's own contributions, the *Consulting Roles Questionnaire* (see Appendix B).

A reflection: the expert who appeals to the imagination

A lot of mythologising takes place among consultants, just like among other professionals: they tell stories in which the merits of consultants are praised in almost superhuman terms. Peter Drucker, in his consultant's autobiography with the apposite title *Adventures of a bystander* (1978), amuses himself with descriptions of heroic consultants. One story[4] is too good to leave out in a chapter about interventions; that of the Dutch expert consultant Willem Paarboom. Of all the myths about consultants, this is one of the most remarkable.

---

4   Which appears on pages 204–212 of that book.

Even to look at, Willem Paarboom was an unusual figure: tall, crow-like, always dressed in black, with four wives who were as alike as peas in a pod, and three children by each wife, who all lived together in a Victorian mansion with countless turrets. As a consultant, he was eccentric and creative, and left behind him a legacy that can still be seen in the world of multinational business.

Paarboom was a financial consultant who was not hired by his clients but started from an inspiration gained from, for example, a newspaper article or something that struck him by chance. He made it a habit to investigate thoroughly something that intrigued him and then to come up with "the solution", a solution that, according to Drucker, was always original, perfect and self-evident – and that no one else had seen before. At that point Paarboom would ring the highest authority in the company, briefly outline what the organisation should do, and then invite himself to come in and explain it in more detail.

Two examples, both dating from 1929, still define the industrial landscape even today: in the US in the late 1920s, Procter & Gamble and Colgate Palmolive – the latter after a recent merger – were expanding rapidly, and Paarboom realised that the time was right to create a food and soap business of similar dimensions in Europe as well. But – then as now – Europe was made up of many smaller countries, with boards of directors that would not be keen to work under each other's authority. Paarboom therefore conceived Unilever as a unique construction: two companies with head offices in London and Rotterdam, one British and the other Dutch, with different shareholders, but headed by the same managing board. Another example is the family firm Opel, the largest car manufacturer in Germany in the late 1920s. With a new generation of Opel brothers at the helm, the company did not think itself strong enough to withstand the crisis years. Paarboom realised that neither the German state nor popular sentiment – with memories of the First World War still fresh – would permit the business to be sold to a company from another European country. He therefore devised the highly successful takeover by General Motors in Detroit.

Paarboom was also one of the most anonymous consultants: his business card bore only his name, no address or telephone number. The point was that he found his clients, not the other way round. He had two criteria that always had to be fulfilled: an inescapable profit and a contribution towards the continued existence of the business. "I long ago stopped earning money with my cleverness – now I want to be paid only because I am imparting meaning," commented Paarboom in the 1930s.

A consultant often chooses to develop interventions with greater impact by allowing his role choice to vary over time. In so doing, he intervenes not only in relation to client and problem, but also in relation to the relationship that client and problem have developed with the consultant up to that point. The consultant is, therefore, also active within the transference triangle as described above. With the intervention the consultant suggests that the client develop a "different sort of transference" in this consulting relationship.[5] I distinguish two main ways of varying interventions over time:

1. *"Outside-in" consulting* (movement from left to right in the intervention triangle): here, the consultant chooses increasingly personal interventions over time. For example, he starts with the problem, or with the relationship between the client(s) and the problem, and gradually proceeds to intervene more in relation to the behaviour and attitude of all concerned. It is primarily experienced experts who do this in practice. They have learned, for example, that if they repeat an expert intervention twice and it results in the same impasse twice, there is probably more going on and they should discuss with their client just how the impasse keeps recurring (see also Block, 1981).

2. *"Inside-out" consulting* (movement from right to left in the intervention triangle): here, the consultant selects increasingly implementation- and solution-oriented interventions in the course of time. After laying the foundations in terms of the assumptions, attitudes and behaviours of the client(s), the client and consultant decide to focus more on the significance of these new acquisitions for the problem and the approach to the problem. Often, new insights and skills lead "automatically" to new approaches to the problem – because it is the client who is the biggest empirical expert in the field of the problem. However, it may sometimes be necessary for the consultant to go a step further in the direction of the problem and help the client with specific applications of what he has learned. This applies primarily where the client uses learning as a sort of diversionary tactic and seems to be revelling in the study of all sorts of new perspectives and solutions, but without proceeding to action.

---

5   Compare with the phenomenon of "positive transference" (Freud, 1912a).

A consultant at work

An e-mail interview with Andrew Campbell, director of the Ashridge Strategic Management Centre, a consultant who works in the role of process manager for many executive boards.

How would you describe your own "added value" in working with executive boards?
I work with senior executives mainly to facilitate their thinking about strategy or organisation issues. I add value if I help my client improve the quality of thinking about strategy or organisation, or if I build extra energy for action by
- creating greater belief that the plan is good;
- facilitating more consensus;
- helping those resisting the plan to reduce their resistance.

How do you intervene?
Mostly my work involves discussions with the client, data collection interviews with a range of managers and facilitation of some decision process, usually a few meetings between the most senior managers. During this process my main contribution is to ensure that the thinking remains strategic. This mainly involves making sure that the criteria used for selecting between alternative strategies are appropriately strategic, thus that
- the implications for the structure of the market are considered;
- the implications for competitive advantage and likely reactions of competitors are considered;
- the resources needed to execute the plan are considered and managers do not assume that they can easily acquire scarce resources from the market place;
- the objectives are built around "value creation" and are not derived from simple gap analysis.

Since my work often involves facilitated discussions rather than data and analysis, I find it helpful to try to lay out the areas of decision choice and the likely range of choices before the event. Often this is the main agenda for the event: what choices would managers make if they had to make them immediately? By focusing on the areas where they are in disagreement or where I am concerned about the strategic wisdom, I help them to focus their data collection and discussion onto the most controversial issues.

How do you see your own role as a consultant in those assignments?
Often the solution is not complicated but managers have become fixated with growth or earnings per share or other less relevant criteria. Sometimes

a senior manager has become committed to a less than ideal strategy and needs a process to help him or her let go.

Most often I feel like a friend more than an advisor. It is easy for me to say things that others have become reluctant to say because of past interactions. I think clients view me as a catalyst. The best clients know what my biases are and use me when they want an outcome that I am likely to be biased towards. Then the client and I are working towards the same solution, but often without pre-discussing it. For example in one situation the client had decided that there was not enough synergy between her businesses and she would probably need to break up the group. She therefore asked me to run a workshop to explore the potential for synergy with her managers. Predictably, the outcome was that very little synergy could be identified. This gave her the mandate to start discussing demerger plans.

Would you say you have "power" in the organisations that you work for, through their executive boards?
I do not think I have any power over the final decisions that are made. However, during the process I often have process power. For example, I can ask a group to do almost anything by way of preparation or syndicate work and they will usually do it without questions. I can ask any question and expect it to be answered. I can interrupt the client and ask him or her to behave differently. However, I have no power over the outcome of the process. This can be frustrating. When a client is committed to a plan of action that I think is foolhardy or insufficiently ambitious, I can point out my concerns, I can even jump up and down and wave my arms, but it makes no difference. I can only succeed if I alter what is in the heads of those with power.

For example at a recent meeting, I was trying to get the CEO to commit to making a decision and announcing it before Christmas. This was needed because other managers were depending on his decision to be able to get other things done. However, he just stone-walled me, in the nicest possible way, saying, "Andrew, I know you are trying to get me to commit to do this by Christmas. But I am just not ready."

I don't believe this work is any different at other levels in the organisation: clients will have to decide what they are going to do and the consultant helps them with that. I do notice differences between having one single client and working with a committee. In a committee situation or when I have a client that is not part of the committee, I can become more part of the politics of that team.

The art of intervening

A term that often crops up in connection with intervening is *resistance*, meaning resistance on the part of the client *vis-à-vis* the intervention. Interventions can apparently create resistance. Most handbooks go on to examine resistance phenomena and ways of combating resistance (for example, Block, 1981, devotes two of his best chapters to resistance). However, "resistance" is a rather unfortunate choice of word, which seems to assume that the client is protesting against something that has been introduced in his own best interests. It is as if he suddenly has one more problem (the original problem *and* resistance to the solution to the original problem). The word almost suggests that the client is reacting ungratefully to a gift that has been specially tailored to his needs.

Since the consultant has become part of a triangle with the client from the first interventions, any resistance that may occur is a jointly created phenomenon. Resistance is usually just as recognisable, therefore, in the consultant as in the client: the consultant shows just as much resistance towards this "difficult client" as the client shows towards this "difficult advice". Perhaps the older meaning of "electrical resistance" can still shed the most light on the subject: narrowing, less permeability, tensions and concomitant development of heat in the *connection* between consultant and client. It is good to realise that "resistance" is a word used by the consultant, and that the word is often used after a (not entirely successful) intervention; an intervention for which the consultant is at least partly responsible. For example, in an attempt at fearless speech, he has failed to maintain the connection with the client.

It is important, of course, to be alert and sensitive to potential tensions in the relationship between client and consultant, and to recognise resistance as early as possible. That will give consultant and client time to make adjustments.

From the appearance of resistance we can infer three recommendations for intervening:
1. Slowing down the intervention;
2. Being receptive to the response;
3. Reinforcing the connection with the client.

It may be a good idea to discuss the resistance itself, in order to bring up the subject of the friction within the connection itself and to use this conversation to reinforce the connection.

The more responsibility we can give to the client in interventions, the better. If a client thinks of, realises or initiates something himself, the impact is immeasurably greater than when the consultant thinks of the same thing and proposes it to the client. By slowing down interventions, we invite clients to complete them themselves – or to reject them in a timely manner if they are not relevant. The three recommendations above lead directly to two criteria by which the success of interventions can be judged:
1. *The autonomy of the client* and the degree to which the client develops the intervention himself, makes it his own or attributes it to himself;
2. *The depth of the connection*, where the client shows that he is now closer to and has more confidence in the consultant.

The following *intervention models* show how this can be put into practice. Clearly, an intervention model is actually an entire consulting process in miniature – with entry, exploration, intervention, consolidation and letting go in a pocket-size edition. The question here is: how can we structure that mini-consulting process?

a   Lewin model

This is the most classical of all intervention models, introduced by Kurt Lewin (1951) with the words *unfreeze – change – refreeze*:

1.	*Stopping the clock and letting go* Requesting time and space for "something new". Sometimes it is the client who stops the clock and asks what the consultant thinks of it all.
2.	*Intervening* The consultant tries out "something new" and contributes new ideas or approaches, for example. The client finds something to his liking in it.
3.	*Consolidating* Consultant and client endeavour to make progress in the new direction, for example, by creating supports for it.

b Meeting-of-minds model

A similar model to Lewin's, but with more slowing down. This approach works especially well in groups, where the task is to take several people "along with you" in the intervention. The consultant uses an inquiring style rather than a problem-solving or prescriptive style. There is a natural progression from perspective-forming to opinion-forming to decision-making:

1.	*Preparation* Crucial step in which the consultant realises that he is going to try something. *Interventions*: clearing one's throat, starting to speak and perhaps interrupting the flow of the conversation.
2.	*Recognition* [Perspective-forming I] Say what triggers you to speak, what strikes you. "I notice that we're always jumping from one topic to another", "We don't seem to be managing to get to where we want to be", "Do you also notice a lack of energy in the room?" This is best done as carefully and openly as possible. Bear in mind that if you are trying to arrive at a common perspective, it is not a good idea to impose your perspective from the outset. Sometimes the most cautious comment is the best: "Something is the matter, but what?" Try to speak as neutrally as possible, non-verbally as well – in tone of voice and attitude. *Interventions*: showing something of what you are thinking here and now.
3.	*Designation* [Perspective-forming II] Establish whether the other party or parties is/are prepared to investigate what is the matter. "Do you notice it too?", "What strikes you?", "What do you think is the matter?", etc. Still neutral, non-judgemental, drawing up an inventory. *Interventions*: asking open questions and listening.
4.	*Exploration* [Opinion-forming I] Try to compare different opinions. Investigate the effects of what is happening. See how things are going and what people think. "Because we've spent so long on this one point, we're getting bogged down", "I notice that I am having trouble concentrating as a result", "In my view we've been going too long without a break", etc. *Interventions*: leading the exploration, summarising frequently.
5.	*Choosing a direction* [Opinion-forming II] Often, it is only now that a group is sufficiently focused to be interested in a proposal. Provided you can do it inquiringly and openly: "What can we do to move on from here?", "I think it will work better if we . . . What do you think?" *Interventions*: making a procedural proposal, and continuing to ask questions.
6.	*Changing* [Decision-making] Now the time has come to collect together the proposals and take a joint decision as a group. If you have a proposal yourself, now is the time to submit it. *Interventions*: summarising, speaking fearlessly.

c U model

(see U-METHOD in De Haan, 2004b)

This model goes one step further and attempts to anchor the intervention in underlying assumptions. Instead of answering immediately or intervening on the basis of the issue under discussion, the consultant first investigates the underlying questions or assumptions and attempts to get to grips with them. This model is a good example of *outside-in consulting*.

1.	*Stopping the clock* Requesting time and space for "something new". Sometimes it is the client who stops the clock and asks what the consultant thinks.
2.	*Reflecting* Consultant and client look together at what is the matter.
3.	*Underlying assumptions* Which assumptions are playing a role in the background here?
4.	*Tenable assumptions* Which assumptions are actually tenable and which are less appropriate here?
5.	*Re-description and conversion* How does the situation appear with the new, tenable assumptions? What does this mean for the future?
6.	*Evaluation* Was this a meaningful and helpful interruption? What have we gained from it?

d Ironic model

Another way of conducting a deeper exploration and at the same time speaking fearlessly and ambiguously. See also Chapter 4 and the IRONIC METHOD in De Haan & Burger (2004).

1.	*Presentation of the problem* Consultant and client start with an explicit question or problem.
2.	*Reformulation as a dilemma* The consultant attempts – at least for himself – to reformulate the issue as a dilemma, in which an internal contradiction or discrepancy comes to the surface: "The client wants to . . . , but feels held back by . . ." or "The client wants to put an end to . . . but is aware that . . ."
3.	*The ironic intervention* The ironic communication itself. This can consist of a strong emphasis on an aspect of the story that the consultant wants to query. Alternatively, the consultant can contribute his own point of view and place it in a different perspective at the same time. Example: "If I understand you correctly, you want both to introduce a completely new structure *and* to avoid any sacrifice in efficiency – that seems a lot to ask."
4.	*Working through* The consultant monitors the client's response attentively and tries to facilitate this response as much as possible, by means of encouragements, open questions or summaries. The consultant will summarise the client's response to the ironic intervention as far as possible, without removing the ambiguity of the irony.

e Triangle model

(see Malan, 1995, and compare with the LADDER METHOD in De Haan & Burger, 2004)

The objective of all interventions in this model[6] is to deepen the connection or contact with the client and to increase understanding of the client's contribution. The consultant does not intervene with solutions or proposals, but does attempt to place the entire conflict triangle on the table – so another example of *outside-in consulting*. Interestingly, only the client can say how deep we can go in this form of consulting, so the consultant must be prepared and able to follow him to that level (see also the more detailed example in the Epilogue).

---

6   An example of the use of this model is given in the Epilogue.

1.	*Summary including defensive behaviour* The consultant starts with a summary of what has just been said, including all the hurdles and problems and, as far as possible, what the consultant sees as possible defences: defence mechanisms used in order to avoid facing certain aspects: "So you try to think about it as little as possible", or "So you delegate this job to someone else."
2.	*Check* The consultant takes time to check whether the client sees and recognises the same thing. This can be done by stopping for a moment and waiting for the other person's response, or by asking whether the client identifies with the summary.
3.	*Interpretation: underlying tension* The consultant gives an interpretation of the underlying emotion and tension and attempts, preferably with the help of the other person or persons, to summarise the emotions or anxieties that are present, the emotions that the defence mechanism has replaced, as it were: "Is it difficult to . . . ?", "Is there a fear of . . . ?", or "Do you define the situation as . . . ?"
4.	*Check* The consultant takes the time to check whether the client sees and recognises the same thing. This can be done by stopping for a moment and waiting for possible responses, or by continuing to ask whether the client identifies with the underlying anxiety.
5.	*Interpretation: underlying impulse or emotion* The consultant gives another interpretation, this time of an underlying need, emotion or impulse: "What's bringing about this tension?", "What need makes the defensive behaviour necessary?", "What unpleasant emotion or underlying impulse is taken away by this behaviour?", or "I wonder if it might be the case that . . ."
6.	*Check* The consultant takes time to check with the client whether he sees and recognises the same thing. In this step that should result in a deepening of the connection, because the entire conflict triangle is now explicit and shared by client and consultant.

f   Inside-out model

The goal of this intervention is to bridge the gap between thoughts, intentions or reflections and consequences for practice, therefore the goal is to help prepare for action. This is a good example of *inside-out consulting*, which is particularly useful where there are impasses or long periods of reflection and contemplation, without any move towards action.

1.	*Summarising* The consultant starts with a summary of the conversation up to that point.
2.	*Shifting perspective* The consultant shifts the perspective from the summary or presentation of the problem to the significance of that summary for subsequent actions, preferably in the form of a question: a. [if the summary contains a problem] "How exactly does that appear in practice?", "Imagine I am in that situation, what happens then? What would I notice?" b. [if the summary contains an obstacle or objection] "What if that obstacle is overcome?", "Imagine that objection is not relevant, how would things look then?" c. [if the summary contains a proposal or reflection] "How does that translate to practice?", "How would that look exactly?" Often it is necessary to go through all of a, b and c in this step.
3.	*Preparing courses of action* Consultant and client ask themselves where they go from here and what action will follow from this thinking, and make arrangements accordingly.

The powerless consultant

As a management consultant my position is officially neutral; it does not command or attract much power. People are willing to pay money for my involvement and then find themselves in the role of client or sponsor. They have some power over me as a result, but only insofar as the assignment itself is concerned. And at the "home base" from which I work, I am only one of 60 consultants, so I hold no special position of power.

Less officially, and if I am completely honest, my practice is imbued with power. There is the power that I can exert within the client organisation, because I am there on behalf of a powerful sponsor within the same organisation. There is the power of the good reputation of my consulting firm and the associated Business School, which ensures that new clients start out with a high opinion of my potential contribution. There is the power of my CV and the completed assignments within the same firm, a power that says that I "do my job well" and that a request from me must be considered seriously. And I am well aware of the "other side" of power as well: managers who put pressure on me not to be the bearer of bad news, clients who keep me waiting to comply with their part of the agreement or who lose interest and keep me dangling.

Power is a complicated concept which cannot be discussed at length here. Power exists where two or more parties have (partly) conflicting interests and want to (partly) impose their will on each other. There is a clash of interests, or a (potential) conflict. Generally speaking, interests can be handled in the following four ways (according to Baddeley & James, 1987), with *skilful* perhaps being the only one that sounds truly positive:

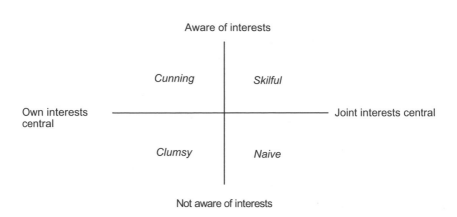

When a consultant intervenes, there is a risk of a "personal interest", in the form of increasingly ambitious desires: that the client should understand and accept the intervention, do something with the intervention and achieve what the intervention intends.

The powerless consultant: officially, the consultant lacks power. But she often speaks on behalf of powerful sponsors who give weight to what she says.

In a pure consulting relationship, it is possible to "intervene without power" – but that succeeds only if there are no conflicts of interest between the client and consultant. The following is a summary of "interests" which I regularly encounter in consultants and clients:

Interests of clients:
- a handle on their own issues;
- a handle on the mix of stability and change;
- perspectives, solutions;
- autonomy;
- influence over the method adopted by their consultant;
- personal development and growth.

Interests of consultants:
- autonomy in choice of method;
- perspectives, solutions;
- satisfied clients;
- finding clever solutions;
- future employment;
- influence over their clients;
- implementation of their own solutions;
- personal development and growth.

It should be clear from this summary that it is possible to have no
conflict of interests between consultant and client, but only if the
client respects the consultant's method and if the consultant
1. does not think he knows best or wants to come across as clever;
2. is not on the lookout for future employment;
3. is not overly attached to his own interventions and solutions.

It is therefore possible to be a "selfless" consultant and so a *powerless*
consultant, who, despite his own powerlessness, can still manage to do
things for the client. The power of this consultant therefore lies in his
lack of desire to have power over anything.

An example

In consultation with my client in a multinational, I inserted a workshop
on "Politics & Power in Organisations" into the programme of a business
course for "high potentials". Only a few weeks later, the client and myself
were summoned to the office of the Human Resources Director. We sat at
an enormous oak table, my client and I on one side and three metres away,
on the other side, the director. His opening words were: "Here in this
organisation we do have power but no politics. And we don't want any
politics. So this section of the programme must be structured differently."
After we had explained the workshop, he proposed a number of changes
and a new title: "Power and Force Fields in Organisations". The conversation rambled on until the true interest and concern of the director finally
emerged: he described how he had been sidelined by political games in a
previous director's position. From the way in which he told his story it was
clear how traumatic it must have been for him. When he had finished his
story, he said, "And the same thing goes on here of course. Perhaps it is a
good thing for our young people to be prepared for it." After that we were
able to revert to the original title of the workshop, and its content.

Conclusion

To end this chapter, it is interesting to pay a visit to a well-known
consultant who was very conscious of power relations: Niccoló
Machiavelli.[7]

---

7   A more detailed study of Machiavelli as a management consultant can be found
    in De Haan (2002). The quotations are almost all derived from English translations
    of Machiavelli (circa 1514, circa 1519). Only the quotation from *Istorie Fiorentine*
    (Machiavelli, 1525) is my own translation.

Exactly 500 years ago, an indefatigable diplomat travels through large parts of what is now the European Union. He acts on behalf of the leaders of one of the most remarkable, richest and smallest, states: Florence. These are the years in which Michelangelo sculpts his David in Florence, and Leonardo paints his Mona Lisa, but Machiavelli never refers to these huge achievements. The achievements he focuses on are within the realm of politics, the complex and opaque politics of the Italy of his time, even more complex and opaque than the politics of today's Italy. Machiavelli visits and negotiates with great men, such as Cesare Borgia ("il Valentino"), the French monarch Louis XII, the German Emperor Maximilian I, Pope Julius II of the House of Della Rovere, and many lesser known rulers.

The more one reads about Machiavelli, the more one grows to like him. For example, the letters that his employees send him as he travels as the ambassador of Florence (Atkinson & Sices, 1996), are extremely touching and provide a picture of his person that is very different from the one history has handed down.[8]

When Machiavelli loses his political influence, Italian literature gains a great author. From the time the Medici family returns to Florence as rulers, in 1512, Machiavelli – advocate of the republic and friend of the escaped "banner-bearer" (*gonfaloniere*) Piero Soderini – is no longer successful in gaining an influential position. He is forced to leave Florence and establishes himself in the village of Sant'Andrea to read the classics[9] and to write. Many of his writings are dedicated to members

---

8 Take, for example, the letter from his colleague Agostino Vespucci (late October 1500): "We are all gripped by a great desire to see you again and long for your pleasurable, witty and happy conversation, which still resounds in our ears and that in our fatigue after long hours of work, still gives us a sense of relief, refreshes and delights us." Or later, the same Vespucci, on 14 October 1502: "I should wish that no one but you would stand by me and be my manager in this chancellery" (Atkinson & Sices, 1996).

9 Machiavelli is not really regarded as belonging to the Florentine humanists, with the group surrounding Lorenzo il Magnifico: Pico della Mirandola, Marsilio Ficino and Angelo Poliziano as its main representatives. Unlike Machiavelli, they read and translated Greek and wrote in Latin. He does, however, enjoy reading the Roman classics, as becomes clear in this well-known quote: "When evening comes, I return to my home, and I go into my study; and on the threshold, I take off my

of the Medici family, in the hope of securing new assignments as a diplomat or of being given a job in government. It is to his failure in securing such assignments (Machiavelli was assigned some minor missions only after 1520) that we owe a wealth of wonderful letters and beautifully written Italian classics.

Machiavelli was a top consultant to the rulers of Florence for many years. From 1498 onwards he held the position of internal consultant because in his role as Second Chancellor he was part of the government. After his dismissal in 1512 he remained politically active, but now more as an external consultant. Nevertheless, Machiavelli hated temporary help and external consultants, just as he hated mercenary troops.[10a] However, he also realised that every leader needs advisers, because a leader can only reflect on his own behaviour through the eyes of an adviser.[b] He warns those who take on consultants about consultants' flattery and toadyism, and loss of respect for the client.[c] He stresses the importance of clear agreements between client and consultant, agreements that make explicit the different responsibilities of leader and consultant. He advises leaders to make sure that their consultants only give solicited advice and to stimulate them to give their opinions openly and frankly.[d]

Leaders should realise, however, that it is the quality of the leader that determines the quality of the consultant, and hence the quality of the advised leadership, unless the leader surrenders completely to the consultant and virtually turns the latter into the leader.[e] The intelligence of a leader can be determined from the consultants he surrounds himself with,[f] and even sound advice from consultants is for a large part dependent on the qualities of the leader himself: it is in fact based on the intelligence of the client.[g]

---

everyday clothes, which are covered with mud and mire, and I put on regal and curial robes; and dressed in a more appropriate manner I enter into the ancient courts of ancient men and am welcomed by them kindly, and there I taste the food that alone is mine, and for which I was born; and there I am not ashamed to speak to them, to ask them the reasons for their actions" (Letter to Francesco Vettori, 1513). For details of the correspondence with Francesco Vettori as a commentary to Machiavelli's political works, the reader is referred to the book *Between Friends* by Najemy (1993).

10 The notes in the form of Latin letters refer to quotes in the two reflections on Machiavelli in this chapter.

A reflection: selection of quotes with Machiavelli's advice to rulers about the best way to deal with internal and external consultants

[a] *This shows, among other things, the reason why mercenary troops are useless, for they have no cause to stand firm when attacked, apart from the small pay which you give them.* [Discorsi I.43]

Those who live in idleness on the abundant revenue derived from their estates (. . .) are a pest in any republic and in any province; but still more pernicious are those who, in addition to the aforesaid revenues, have castles under their command and subjects who are under their obedience. (. . .) Men born in such conditions are entirely inimical to any form of civic government. [Discorsi I.55]

[b] *So, to comprehend fully the nature of the people, one must be a prince, and to comprehend fully the nature of princes one must be an ordinary citizen.* [Il Principe Dedication]

[c] *The only way to safeguard yourself against flatterers is by letting people understand that you are not offended by the truth; but if everyone can speak the truth to you then you lose respect.* [Il Principe XXIII.1]

[d] *So a shrewd prince should adopt a middle way, choosing wise men for his government and allowing only those the freedom to speak the truth to him, and then only concerning matters on which he asks their opinion, and nothing else. But he should also question them thoroughly and listen to what they say; then he should make up his own mind, by himself. And his attitude towards his councils and towards each one of his advisors should be such that they will recognise that the more freely they speak out the more acceptable they will be. Apart from these, the prince should heed no one; he should put the policy agreed upon into effect straight away, and he should adhere to it rigidly. Anyone who does not do this is ruined by flatterers or is constantly changing his mind because of conflicting advice: as a result he is held in low esteem. (. . .) A prince must, therefore, always seek advice. But he must do so when he wants to, not when others want him to; indeed, he must discourage everyone from tendering advice about anything unless it is asked for. All the same, he should be a constant questioner, and he must listen patiently to the truth regarding what he has inquired about.* [Il Principe XXIII.2]

[e] *Here is an infallible rule; a prince who is not himself wise cannot be well advised, unless he happens to put himself in the hands of one individual who looks after all his affairs and is an extremely shrewd man. In this case, he may well be given good advice, but he would not last long because the man who governs for him would soon deprive him of his state.* [Il Principe XXIII.4]

[f] *The first opinion that is formed of a ruler's intelligence is based on the quality of the men he has around him. When they are competent and loyal he can always be considered wise, because he has been able to recognise their competence and to keep them loyal.* [Il Principe XXII.1]

[g] *So the conclusion is that good advice, whomever it comes from, depends on the shrewdness of the prince who seeks it, and not the shrewdness of the prince on good advice.* [Il Principe XXIII.4]

On the other hand Machiavelli can well understand the role of consultant to leaders – the role of "management consultant" – if only from being one himself for many years. With his fatalistic spirit he is very sensitive to the risks which threaten a consultant who works closely with a ruler:[h]

- having to bear the (ascribed) responsibility for the consequences of advice, without the accompanying mandate[i] (see also Chapter 8 of this book);
- being evaluated on the eventual outcome, not on the quality of the advice as such, and then not in an even-handed manner in which positives and negatives are weighed against each other;[j]
- being exposed to the constant pressure to be impartial and detached on the one hand and the danger of losing credibility as consultant on the other;[k]
- possibly inviting the damage that can be done by offering sound advice in a fearless manner, but in doing so striking a wrong tone.[l]

From his words, it appears that Machiavelli succeeded in consolidating his position as a consultant amidst the complex political forces of the Florentine rulers for many years, mainly by working discreetly and by not insisting on being the spiritual father of ideas.[m]

A reflection: selection of quotes with Machiavelli's advice to internal and external consultants about the best way to deal with rulers

[h] *What dangers are run by one who takes the lead in advising some course of action; and how much greater are the dangers incurred when the course of action is unusual.* [Discorsi III.35]

[i] *For men judge actions by the result. Hence for all the ill that results from an enterprise the man who advised it is blamed, and, should the result be good, commended; but the reward by no means weighs the same as the loss.* [Discorsi III.35]

[j] *It is not wise to judge things from their effects, because often those things that are well-counselled do not eventually end well, and the things which are ill-advised do have a fortunate ending; therefore, if one praises bad advices for the ending they have had, one only encourages others to err similarly; which is very harmful for republics because usually bad advices are less fortunate; in a similar way that one errs if one criticizes a good counsel because it has an unfortunate effect, because then one takes away courage from citizens to counsel the state and to say what they think.* [Istorie Fiorentine IV.7].

^k *The advisors of a republic and the counsellors of a prince are undoubtedly in a difficult position; for, unless they recommend the course which in their honest opinion will prove advantageous to that city or to that prince regardless of consequences, they fail to fulfil the duties of their office, while, if they recommend it, they are risking their lives and endangering their position, since all men in such matters are blind and judge advice to be good or bad according to the result.* [Discorsi III.35]

^l *We see, then, how harmful the Romans thought it to calumniate others or to reproach them for a shameful deed, as has been said, for then there is nothing that inflames the mind more, or accuses greater indignation, whether the taunt be true or be said in jest, "For smart sayings, when they border on the truth, leave a bitter taste behind them."* [Discorsi II.26] Here, at the end, Machiavelli cites Tacitus' Annals: *Nam facetiae asperae, quando nimium ex vero traxere, acrem sui memoriam relinquunt.*

^m *Nor do I see any way of avoiding either the infamy or the danger than by putting the case with moderation instead of assuming responsibility for it, and by stating one's views dispassionately and defending them alike dispassionately and modestly; so that, if the city or the prince accepts your advice, he does so of his own accord, and will not seem to have been driven to it by your importunity. (. . .) And, though, in the case we have taken, there is lacking the glory which comes to the man who in opposition to the many, alone advocates a certain course which turns out well, it has two advantages. Firstly, it does not entail danger. Secondly, if you tender your advice with modesty, and the opposition prevents its adoption, and, owing to someone else's advice being adopted, disaster follows, you will acquire very great glory.* [Discorsi III.35]

We can imagine powerlessness at the mid-point of a sliding scale with "dependence" and "powerplay" at either end. Dependent behaviour means going along with resistance or coalitions within the client or client organisation, and powerplay means manifesting personal interests oneself or making use of a position with power. The consultant attempts to achieve mastery by staying away from these extremes and feeling comfortable in the middle zone, applying selflessness and powerlessness in a variety of situations.

Summary: intervening and power

Intervening means stepping in. Intervening begins from the very first moment of contact between consultant and client. The consultant steps in in a number of ways:
1. Between client and problem, with a new perspective on both ("basic intervention triangle");
2. Between different clients, with a mediating role ("mediation triangle");
3. Between existing patterns of behaviour of the client ("transference triangle") – sometimes between dramatic, ingrained patterns ("drama triangle");
4. Between tensions, impulses and emotions within the client in relation to those patterns of behaviour ("conflict triangle").

The art of intervening is to become sufficiently involved when stepping in, and at the same time to retain one's own detachment and independence. Criteria which determine the success of interventions are the autonomy of the client and the depth of the connection between client and consultant.

In intervening between client and problem, the consultant can choose different possible focuses, and therefore different **roles**:
1. focused on the problem: the **expert** contributes knowledge and knowledge-based solutions;
2. focused on the connection between client and problem: the **process manager** is concerned with this connection and with progress;
3. focused on the behaviour and approach of the client: the **developer** suggests new approaches and influences by means of feedback;
4. focused on the client himself: the **coach** opens up new perspectives and asks in-depth questions.

Movement between these views is found in **inside-out** and **outside-in** intervening.

As an aid the consultant uses – consciously or unconsciously – an **intervention model**, such as the **Lewin model**, the **Meeting-of-minds model**, the **U model**, the **Ironic model**, the **Triangle model** or the **Inside-out model**.

Intervening is an action which may trigger a reaction. The consultant is therefore not necessarily free of the resistance and of the politics and power in organisations, even though a **selfless and powerless intervention** is often more effective than when the consultant
1. thinks he knows better or wants to come across as clever;
2. is on the look out for future employment;
3. is overly attached to his own interventions and solutions.

7
Characteristics of Consolidating

In the fourth phase of consulting, the phase of consolidating, the consultant's aim is mainly *to facilitate what is working at this moment*. In a successful consulting process, the consultant can now lean back a little, do more self-monitoring without too much self-directing, and focus exclusively on the changes taking place for his client. The consultant gradually becomes more like a member of the audience in a theatre; observing what is taking place on the stage, perhaps identifying with the protagonist and pondering what exactly is going on. The most important question is still: "What belongs to me, and what belongs to my client?" This enables the consultant to direct his own interventions in such a way that what belongs to him is gradually reduced and what belongs to his client is gradually increased.

So much for a successful consulting process. What about a less successful one? A less successful assignment perhaps requires new exploration and new interventions, i.e. a return to earlier phases, although it is also my view that consultants who have already tried once in vain are unlikely in this stage to achieve anything more with their change-oriented interventions. The outcome must "belong to the client" and, if that does not happen, there is little point in persisting.

After the experiences in the previous phase, it is usually clear to all concerned that client and consultant have come upon new possibilities and that the client has been invited to see or handle things differently. The choice is up to the client who has, roughly speaking, three options:

1. The client perseveres with his old approach. In this case he will be less open to the consultant and may adopt a rigid approach or express decreasing interest. The consultant would do well to move on as quickly as possible to the final phase, that of evaluation and departure.

2. The client finds a new way of looking at things or a new strategy of his own. Now it depends on the circumstances whether the consultant can still make a contribution. In any case, the independence and energy of the client greatly increase the chance of success, because the client has assumed responsibility. It is best for the consultant to put his own vanity aside and not allow himself to be led by a feeling of being unappreciated. On the contrary, even though things are not going entirely according to the consultant's plan, there is ample reason to be satisfied with a successful assignment, however it was completed.

3. The advice is received and implemented with enthusiasm. The consultant is usually invited to assist the client in consolidating the changes. He will do so with pleasure and will be delighted to explain his proposals from the previous phase again or to adapt them to deal with more specific problems. However, this welcome development also carries a risk with it, namely the risk of unnecessary and even harmful mutual dependence between client and consultant, where the consultant needs the client for his own success story, while the client needs the consultant in order to maintain the new situation.

Whatever understanding or division of responsibilities develops in this phase, it has two characteristic features:

1. The client becomes more independent and starts to develop more autonomously.

2. For the consultant, this phase is already influenced by themes of the final phase, that of evaluation and completion.

Consolidating: now the client "makes off with" the outcomes of the consulting process and assumes increasing responsibility, either to do something new or to keep things the same. At the same time, the consultant moves towards a more detached position.

The responsibility of consultant and client in this phase is therefore a genuine involvement in the other person, but without doing something for the other person that he can do himself.

If the consulting process has progressed successfully, something has been changed for the better in the client's situation and the consultant has the opportunity to observe that change at first hand. The difference may initially be very small, confined to specific moments and situations, fragile or fluctuating, perhaps with frequent relapses into the old situation or old behaviour. Sometimes, on the other hand, there may be "transformational" changes, where the change is overwhelming and all-encompassing from the start. However, this sort of change is very rare in practice and often exists more in the fantasies of client and consultant than in reality. Reflecting the client's frequent relapses and

frequent temptation to revert to doing things the old way, the consultant too often experiences both a relapse and a temptation at this point.
The relapse usually arises from the fact that he is less in charge and
less pivotal, and the temptation, in my experience, can move the
consultant into two directions:

1. A temptation to carry on with successful intervening as in the
    previous phase, for example by repeatedly explaining what is
    best for the client. In practice, this is often counterproductive
    even if the client accepts it, because the consultant continues to
    "make a difference" when the client is already capable of doing
    it himself.

2. A temptation to leave too early and to move on to different, "more
    interesting" consulting assignments, while the client still has a
    need for reflection and the consultant's supportive interventions.
    The consultant sometimes feels rejected, which may be a misin-
    terpretation of the fact that the client is now starting to do
    things more autonomously. An unconscious, automatic reaction
    to this feeling of being rejected is, as is well known (see, for
    example, Malan, 1995), to take one's leave and do the rejecting
    oneself.

Usually, there is still a lot for the consultant to do in this phase, and
new interventions to make, directed towards "encouraging", or "consolidating" the changes. The subtle art of letting go and bidding fare-
well also begins in this phase, where the consultant tries, gradually and
elegantly, to move away from the centre of the change.

In the next chapter I want to look at a concept that has everything to
do with bringing about and consolidating change, the concept of
responsibility. After providing some background to the concept and a
reflection on the difficulty of really coming to grips with "who is
responsible for what" and what exactly that means, we look at the
responsibility of the consultant in this phase and at the ways in
which the consultant can ensure that the client can look after
himself.

♫ **Summary: characteristics of consolidating**

> **Consulting** is a temporary collaborative relationship between client and consultant, the objective of which is an improvement in the client's fortunes.
>
> Consulting is also an attitude or state of mind on the part of the consultant, which takes the following forms:
> 1. **Fearless speech**: open and honest, without fear of the consequences;
> 2. **Exploration**: listening to and interpreting what the client introduces;
> 3. **Self-monitoring and self-directing**: the ability to examine and guide the consulting activity itself from a different, sometimes more objective, perspective;
> 4. **Facilitating change**: being present during change, respecting the autonomous nature of change;
> 5. **Letting go** of what belongs to the client, practising detachment *vis-à-vis* the change that, as a consultant, one has become personally involved in.

In the fourth phase, that of **consolidating**, the art of consulting appears to consist primarily of facilitating change.

The consultant is **present** in the situation as an outsider, **reflects** on the situation, and **helps** with supportive interventions.

The client starts to develop greater autonomy and independence, while the consultant is already looking forward to the next phase, that of completion and departure.

8
Consolidating and Responsibility

*Thus, our age is sufficiently depressed to know that there is
something called responsibility and that this means something.
Therefore, although everyone wants to rule,
no one wants to have responsibility.*

(Kierkegaard, *The Tragic in Ancient Drama Reflected in
the Tragic in Modern Drama*, in: *Either/Or*, 1843)

The responsibility of the consultant

In consolidating a change, the consultant seeks a balance in his own
involvement and interventions, in a subtle dance between "too much"
and "too little". In being present and encouraging a change process
that is as autonomous as possible, the consultant attempts to share his
own responsibility with the client as much as possible. The client's
responsibility is primarily to accomplish the change, and that of the
consultant primarily to facilitate the change. These responsibilities
overlap, so it is quite an art for the consultant to contribute significantly and at the same time not to take over.

The responsibility of a consultant is certainly something special. Like
a manager, a consultant bears responsibility for other people. In the
case of the manager we can say that he bears "final responsibility", so
is ultimately accountable for whatever happens in his part of an organisation. His staff assume parts of that responsibility only on a temporary
basis. In other words, the staff help the manager bear his many
responsibilities.

It would be so easy if we could say something similar about the consultant: that a consultant bears responsibility for tasks A, B and C, and
that he does his job better the more he brings those tasks to a successful
conclusion and assumes more responsibility for them. But it is not as
simple as that. The consultant's responsibility is to help the client,
which can actually be less successful if the consultant takes more – or
indeed sole! – responsibility. This is demonstrated most succinctly in

the definition of consulting as the *facilitating of change*, a definition often used to describe this phase. If the consultant remains the "owner" of the change, there is a high risk that everything will unravel when the consultant leaves – and that is not a successful outcome for client or consultant.

Why does anything come about?

Conversations about responsibility in organisations often appear incomprehensible. The exact answer to the question "Who precisely is responsible for what?" remains shrouded in a thick mist, perhaps because:

- there is a lack of agreement on what exactly is happening or needs to be done;
- there is a lack of agreement on exactly who should be doing what;
- the parties involved – all too human and all too political! – seek to lay responsibility as far as possible outside themselves;
- there is a lack of understanding about why and with whose help something comes about.

Let us take the last of these first. If we have a clear answer to the question why something comes about, we are better able to determine and define responsibilities.

One of the oldest, most accepted and clearest answers to the question "Why does anything come about?" is given by Aristotle in his model of working and changing. He says that there are four possible answers to that question:[1]

1. Where it comes from, or the basic material. Traditionally, this is called the *material cause* or *causa materialis*. This refers to "that out of which a thing comes to be", or that which contains the final outcome within itself, as a potentiality. Example: "Why was the go-ahead given?" "Because everyone was present and we found all of the necessary information in the documents."

---

1   This model, which is known as the "doctrine of the four causes", recurs at various points in the works of Aristotle, e.g. in his *Analytica Posteriora, Fysica* and *Metafysica* (Aristotle, 4th century BC). Aristotle's own terms are *hulè* (material), *eidos* (form, idea), *kinoun* (impulse to change) and *telos* (aim). And the term used by Aristotle for causes (*aitiai*) can be translated equally well by responsibilities.

2. What serves as a model, or the best result on paper. Traditionally, this is called the *formal cause* or *causa formalis*. This refers to the strategy or plan used as the basis for carrying out the work. Example: "Why did we launch that new campaign?" "Because our new strategy makes it clear that we have to come across differently."
3. The work that is needed to achieve it, or the impetus for the change. Traditionally, this is called the *efficient cause* or *causa efficiens*. This refers to the effort that is required in order to bring something into being. Example: "Why is this finished already?" "Because they worked really hard on it in recent weeks."
4. The objective which is envisaged, or the final result. Traditionally, this is called the *final cause* or *causa finalis*. This refers to the reason why you are doing something, i.e. the best outcome in reality. Example: "Why is he out running in the park?" "For the good of his health!"

In modern "business speak" we talk of responsibility for the *input* (material cause), for the *strategy* or *design* (formal cause), for the *job* (efficient cause) and for the *output* (final cause).

Four areas of responsibility: the underlying plan, the incoming documents, the actual work and the outgoing documents.

All four of these components are necessary in order to make something or to change something. Aristotle cites the example of the building of a house, where:
1. the material cause is the building materials, plus tools and labour;
2. the formal cause is the building plan, and the architect's drawing;
3. the efficient cause is the decision and the impulse to build, and the building work itself; and
4. the final cause is the finished house which is the ultimate aim of all these efforts.

Another example can be derived from organisational change. For example, if an organisation wants to move a production facility to another country, it will need:
1. knowledge, materials and labour on the spot;
2. a clear plan with a schedule and a design plus a strategy of the new production site;
3. initiative on the part of the management and effort on the part of many people concerned;
4. a guiding principle based on the ultimate advantages of the final result.

It is not difficult to make this distinction for every job and for every change and to identify the key "players" in each of the four categories. Using a play on his own name (*telos ariston*), Aristotle writes in the *Ethica Eudemia* (1218b) that the final cause is the best because it inspires and, as it were, attracts the change. According to Aristotle, the final cause is the only one which does not generate resistance. In working and changing, the final result is paramount: after all, that is what you are doing it for!

Aristotle's model is a fairly complete overview of aspects, explanations, causes or principles of work and change. If we look now at the problem of responsibility, we see that there is always a person with final responsibility, or an owner, for each of these areas. Often the top management is the owner of the formal cause: the plan, the strategy, the budget. Depending on the work, the client, customer or shareholder is the owner of the result to be delivered, i.e. the final cause. Often, the same person is the owner of several aspects and we can therefore put the same name against several causes, as Aristotle himself points out. An example is the attainment of the same performance level as last year in a personal development plan: here, material, formal and final cause are the same person (first, potentially able to do it, then as a model from the previous year, and finally representing the ultimate performance) – and the efficient cause is the same person working to achieve this result.

Problems arise where the owners of different aspects are different people. For example, if I am unable to complete a project on time as the project leader, the main obstacle being that department heads have not given me access to enough project workers, whose responsibility is that? In that case I am the owner of the efficient cause: my task is to do the actual work with my project team. But if my project team is not up to strength, I do not have enough "material". This material cause may come under the authority of other people, managers within the organisation, who are telling their people, for example, that they needn't place a high priority on my project. Or I am the director of a division that has been instructed by management to grow by 20% this year, although this strikes me as impossible in a shrinking market with the same products and unchanged marketing budgets. Whose fault is it that I am not managing? Who is responsible? Such problems are all too familiar within and between organisations.

Aristotle was well aware of the implications of his model for looking at the causes of success and failure. He cites as an example – considering the efficient cause – the criticism of the helmsman after a shipwreck, and the equal praise for the same helmsman after a safe voyage. In the *Politica* (1331b29) Aristotle applies his principles to the government of a state. He says that the government of a state will be good where the choice of plan and the aim of the activity (formal and final cause) are in the same hands as the choice of the activities to achieve that aim (efficient cause). In such a case, it is only possible that someone may not complete the activity and can be brought to account. Things become more complicated – and this is often the case, unfortunately, in business organisations – where we do not have complete control over all four areas. I distinguish three frequently occurring instances:

1. *Responsibility without mandate*, or doing the work without a handle on the formal cause. We are the owner of the efficient cause, the material cause and the final cause, but are unable to influence the formal cause. Here, we bear responsibility for a "piece of work" and are held

accountable for the result – but we have no, or too little, influence on the actual task to be done. This can work well if the task is easy, but when someone else who does have a mandate tightens the thumbscrews, there is too little opportunity to make adjustments.

2. *Mandate and responsibility, but insufficient grip on materials*, or doing the work without a handle on the material cause. We are the owner of the efficient case, the formal cause and the final cause, but are unable to influence the material cause. Now we can share in the drafting of our own plan, we have control of the execution and are held accountable for the result, but we lack influence over the material or the people we have to work with (see also the example of the project manager above). This is generally a less serious situation than the previous one, because we can draft our plans more modestly and so often lower the expectations of our clients.

3. *Mandate without responsibility*, or doing the work without a handle on the final cause. We are the owner of the material, formal and efficient cause, but do not have to bear ownership of the final result. This is a position of luxury, in which we have a handle on the entire process, but whatever we do, we will not be held accountable. This is the point at which power begins to corrupt, as in an absolute monopoly without critical customers.

Authority and responsibility

In business organisations "responsibility" is an important theme nowadays, one which is often dissected in detail in appraisals and when something goes wrong. However, managers and staff often underestimate the importance of responsibility and the problematic issues which attach to the distribution of ownership between different parties. Some examples:

- Whose responsibility is it really when something goes wrong in the execution of a task?
- Is the worker's manager ultimately responsible – so then, "where does the buck stop" and what does that mean?
- How about "political responsibility" in business organisations: when can you be held accountable for a failure – for example, for unexpectedly high losses – even though you personally played no direct part in the failure?
- What does it mean to assume the "right" responsibility: where is the right middle way between *wearing oneself out* under the burden of too much responsibility and *avoiding* responsibility?

This is not all there is to say on the subject of responsibility. Perhaps the most important thing still remains unsaid. I still have to make a distinction between *intrinsic* and *extrinsic* responsibility. Up to this point I have been talking about the *extrinsic* responsibilities in working and organising: the aspects for which workers and their managers must assume formal responsibility. I have not yet said anything about the actual ability to take on and bear those responsibilities, and even to go a step further if there are reasons to do so. That *intrinsic* responsibility is the *dedication* to one's own (extrinsic) area of responsibility, including the ability to go a step further – outside that area – if it becomes clear that carrying on within one's own sphere of responsibility will lead to unsatisfactory results. Thierry (1965) takes us to the core of the word responsibility[2] and defines it as our ability to *respond* to an appeal. When someone sees a burning cigarette lying in a wastepaper basket and walks on, he has behaved irresponsibly, because he has not given the correct response to the situation.

Another, more extreme, example, which is still fresh in the Dutch national memory, is the behaviour of the Dutch battalion Dutchbat in Srebrenica, after the Bosnian enclave had been surrounded and captured by the Bosnian-Serb army. Again and again, the Dutch troops fulfilled all of their agreed responsibilities to the letter, while at the same time it became ever clearer to them that not only was the "safe enclave" becoming increasingly unsafe but that serious human rights infringements were taking place right under their noses. The official NIOD (Netherlands Institute for War Documentation) report on Srebrenica contains the following line: "They carried out their duties, but that had far from the intended effect." Srebrenica shows precisely what a lack of intrinsic responsibility can lead to. Not going the extra mile while simply carrying out the task for which you have extrinsic responsibility may end in total failure.

Without intrinsic responsibility, without personal involvement, without *dedication* to the responsibility associated with a particular position, it is impossible to bring about things that would not happen automatically anyway – "automatically" meaning in this case: because

---

2   Although the derivation must be sought in the French *responsabilité* and so in the Latin *spondere*, which means to pledge or solemnly promise. *Respondere* means to vouch for or guarantee something.

someone else takes responsibility for them. Without this intrinsic involvement or dedication, I believe it is impossible to fulfil the role of professional or manager in a creative manner, a manner that makes a difference within the organisation. The taking of responsibility calls for more coordination and perseverance than one might think. There are all sorts of obstacles, internal barriers as well as external impediments. Moreover, intrinsic responsibility is, in my experience, one of the most difficult things to learn, and the ability to take responsibility appears to change little in the course of a human life. Taking responsibility depends greatly on attitude and personality, both of which are very difficult to change, even if one is motivated to try. In addition, any responsibility assumed is quickly dropped under conditions of stress and external pressure, though it is in precisely those circumstances that continuing to take responsibility is so important.

In general, for every "piece of work" we attempt to find an agreement between our (extrinsic) *responsibility* and our *mandate*, so we try to be the owner of both the final cause and the formal cause. We want the results for which we can be held accountable to be consistent with the authority to be able to influence those same results. As a manager, but also as a consultant and as someone who executes tasks, my own responsibility should correspond with my mandate, so that responsibility taken and given, in other words the responsibility to carry out the job (material, formal and efficient cause) and the responsibility for the job carried out (final cause), are consistent with each other.

In organisations, there are often considerable tensions regarding the lack of consistency between responsibility and authority:
1. *Responsibility without mandate* often arises because the higher management is only prepared to share its own authority with others to a limited extent or does not assume certain responsibilities – such as for problem-solving, decision-making or appointing staff. These responsibilities then devolve "automatically" to middle management, which becomes overburdened on account of their intrinsic responsibility. The worst thing about this situation is that these overburdened managers are often unable to solve their own problems because they lack the necessary authority. For this reason, business consultants often argue against this structure and attach great importance to the delegation of a genuine mandate. An extreme example of the taking of responsibility without mandate is

the phenomenon of the "whistle-blower", the professional who exposes an undesirable practice that goes far beyond his own sphere of responsibility.

2. *Mandate without responsibility* is a form of abuse of power that we encounter regularly in higher managers and sometimes also in support staff. They issue directives and demand all sorts of results from others, for which they themselves cannot be held directly accountable. This phenomenon of taking insufficient responsibility for one's own authority is also increasingly common among younger managers. They are keen to progress as quickly as possible through as many posts as possible, in order to gain experience in different aspects of management. They regard more than four years in the same post as a blot on their CV. As a result, they spend less and less time in any one post and never have to clean up the mess left behind by their decisions. One can argue that some of these successful "movers and shakers" never carry any real responsibility.

It is difficult to say which of these two is more harmful for the effectiveness of an organisation. Perhaps the latter, because those left behind cannot hold anyone responsible for the damage caused. In the first case, the authority remains firmly in the hands of the top management or the shareholders, who can therefore also be held accountable.

A reflection: without responsibilities to be reduced to "nothing"

Interestingly, Shakespeare often writes about situations in which a leader is responsible for his decisions but lacks the necessary authorisations, mandates or resources. The leader in question is then responsible without authority and often also without the ability to escape his responsibility. Characteristically, in his histories and tragedies Shakespeare shows extreme consequences of the non-agreement of formal cause and final cause, i.e. of authority and responsibility:

1. Responsibility without mandate is the problem of many of Shakespeare's tragic heroes. Examples are Hamlet and King Lear. Hamlet, as the crown prince, does not yet have any authority in Denmark, but immediately in the first act is informed about grievous wrongdoings related to the succession to the throne. At the start of his tragedy King Lear transfers all of his authority to two of his daughters, but then lacks the authority to intervene when things go wrong. See also my more detailed analysis in *The consulting process as drama* (De Haan, 2004a).

2. In the historical tragedy *Richard II*, Shakespeare describes the fate of a
   king who reigns solely on the basis of his "divine authority", but
   without the corresponding personal authority – an extreme example
   of mandate without responsibility (see also Corrigan, 1999). Richard
   II alienates himself completely from his subjects and is ultimately
   deposed with general assent.

Many of Shakespeare's works are concerned with the question of what is
good leadership and how leaders should deal with power, responsibility
and authority. Shakespeare shows us extreme examples, which are also
relevant for consultants towards the end of the consulting process. At that
point a consultant generally has no authority, power or responsibility and
is therefore reduced to "nothing" as far as his role is concerned. Shakespeare's heroes undergo this existential and oppressive experience of being
reduced to nothing and reflect on that state. Andrews (1961) demon-
strates how Shakespeare broaches this topic in many places, and asks why
there is so "much ado about nothing" in his dramas. He finds an answer
in tragedies such as *Coriolanus*, *Richard II* and *Timon of Athens*: time and
time again Shakespeare tells us in so many words that in order to lay strong
foundations for a viable organisation in which people can be responsible
for their actions and deeds, we must first learn to cope with "nothing",
with emptiness, ambiguity, indefiniteness and nihilism. A beautiful expression of this can be found in the final monologue of Richard II, when he
is no longer king and is languishing in prison:

> *Nor I, nor any man that but man is*
> *With nothing shall be pleased, till he be eased*
> *With being nothing.* [*Richard II*, V.5.39]

King Lear is a study of what can come out of that nothing: *Can you make
use of nothing?* (*King Lear*, I.4.139; see also De Haan, 2004a). Coriolanus
and Timon of Athens are also reduced to "nothing" in their respective
tragedies. Timon of Athens, like Richard II, appears in the final act to be
able to learn from his condition of "being nothing":

> *My long sickness*
> *Of health and living now begins to mend*
> *And nothing brings me all things.* [*Timon of Athens*, V.1.187]

The question of personal responsibility – and the question of personal
entrepreneurship – is in essence the question of "What can we do with
nothing?", and even more of "What we can do if we *are* nothing?", if we
are deprived of material, formal and efficient causes (responsibilities), and

also of final causes (authorities). What can we then do "of and by ourselves"? Interestingly, this is also often the situation of the consultant during the consolidation phase: "No one asks me anything any more, no one seems to want anything from me any more . . . How can I do anything that has meaning and imparts meaning, without attracting new responsibilities, so without actually turning back the clock?"

The non-responsible consultant

For organisation consultants, neither of the two dangers mentioned above is theoretical:

1. *Responsibility without mandate* is the burden that every consultant carries with him in a sense, even if this is primarily *intrinsic* responsibility without mandate. A consultant exerts influence only at the request and on the mandate of the client (compare with Weinberg's definition of advice in Appendix A), so he has no direct responsibility for the outcome. The authority remains with the client. This lack of mandate may lead to a "tragic" perception of his profession on the part of the consultant, which I will come to in Chapter 10. Strictly speaking, therefore, the consultant usually has no formal responsibility for the result, but most consultants do not see it that way and actually behave very responsibly.

2. *Mandate without responsibility* is seen primarily in consultants who act as interim managers or as "co-managers" of business units, or else as chairmen of merger committees or "change teams".[3] They taste a pleasure that is rare for consultants: real power over their clients. They easily can, and often unconsciously do, abuse that power. In fact, they are in a position to issue directives without being held accountable for them, especially where they are paid solely on the basis of their own time investment, as is normally the case. For the organisation, the time of reckoning is in the distant future, when the (interim) consultant has already left for the next assignment. Due to the temporary and effort-oriented nature of the consulting contract, these consultants themselves are therefore at no risk of becoming the victim of their interventions: the fact that they are not employed by the organisation makes them virtually invulnerable, which is obviously something to be very aware of and alert about.

---

3 Especially in the case of *process managers* therefore (see Chapters 5 and 6).

In general, client and consultant work with a *shared responsibility*, where the client retains the final mandate. The authority remains with the client. The responsibility of the consultant is often wide in scope to start with and diminishes in the later phases of the consulting assignment: at the start the consultant has to immerse himself in and study the issue and the context, to do research and develop his own vision of the issue, and to intervene in one way or another. In a successful consulting assignment the responsibility of the consultant declines gradually after that, while the client assumes more responsibility for himself, helped by the facilitating contributions of the consultant. As a result, we sometimes see shifts towards other consulting roles, such as that of a process manager or a coach. This is a result of the fact that a consultant can maintain the roles of the process manager and the coach for longer, because they can be fulfilled more easily from the sidelines.

A practical case: responsibility for connection and cohesion

Sometimes I notice that I, as a consultant, do not come on stage until the final phase of the handling of an issue within an organisation, so that I hardly have to assume any responsibility. An organisation is already so thoroughly aware of the problem and has already done so much to combat it, that as a consultant one need only be present in order to achieve the intended results of the project. It is as if the solution has already been found, but the awareness of that solution has not yet sunk in sufficiently. I often have the feeling that I am that caricature of a consultant who requests the client's own watch and then tells him the time (the well-known *bon mot* of Ed Finkelstein in the *New York Times*, April 1979). Ironically, these are often my more successful assignments.

An example is the medium-sized government organisation for which I worked as an organisation consultant for almost four years, at an average of half a consulting day per month. On entry in 1999 the problem was already very clear: a number of years before, a report by a large consultancy had depicted collaboration within the organisation as a "vacuum between large islands" and a "wasteland in which the middle management has lost its way". In addition, the organisation had been placed under the financial supervision of the national government for a number of years, so it was lagging behind in terms of investments in structure and systems and in the development of its professionals.

During the first year there were some changes in the management team which made it possible to steer the organisation more centrally. Our open

Aladdin sessions for managers (in which "the genie was allowed to come out of the bottle"!), our articles in the internal media and the "team-building" activities that we introduced for the whole staff soon proved successful.

My own role in this could best be typified as that of a process manager (see Chapter 5): I sat in on a group of employees from different management levels and sectors that were concerned about the "vacuum" within the organisation. From that group, the Connection & Cohesion Working Group, we organised organisation-wide working conferences and helped managers to develop a shared vision of management within the organisation.

The assignment culminated in an *open space* (Owen, 1997) event for all 80 managers in the organisation, which resulted in a wide range of initiatives. I quote here from an e-mail that I received from my client more than six months after the end of the assignment: "Connection & Cohesion, hmm, it's certainly still going in a way, but quite different from what we ever imagined. A couple of examples: the management circle is still going, under its own steam and quite effectively. That model (self-organised middle management as the driving force of our organisation) is often cited when it comes to boosting new developments we are working on, such as developing social governance or reinforcing our service provision. In that sense we are starting to 'discover' the middle management as a factor. A recurring topic in the organisation is the overly sector- or branch-oriented 'island' atmosphere."

As in many assignments, a lot of our initiatives ran aground.[4] I found it a shame in particular as far as our *survey feedback method* (Baumgartel, 1959) was concerned: series of electronic surveys with the aim of asking all 800 people in the organisation every year how they experienced "connection

---

4   In this connection it is useful to quote from the autobiography of the well-known management consultant and writer Roger Harrison: "Now, as I look back on the projects I have engaged in over the more than thirty-five years I have worked in consulting, research, and management education, I can point to no more than five in which I believe I personally made a significant difference in the life of the organisation, and of those, there were only three where my influence was transformative in the sense that my presence and activities led to changes in significant values, beliefs, and ways of working. Of those three, there was only one in which I believe that the transformation was not reversed later on" (Harrison, 1995, p. 76). I have less experience than Harrison, so I guess these figures are considerably lower in my case.

& cohesion" in their own work. We did not get any further than the baseline survey. As a result, we now don't know whether or not our interventions had any tangible impact on the organisation. I believe that repeating the surveys could have helped us to make the theme more concrete for all involved and to assess in a reliable manner whether or not we had achieved results.

The whole assignment was based on intrinsic responsibility: the Connection & Cohesion group could only exist thanks to the dedication of 10 employees from all levels of the organisation. I managed to take on very little responsibility but nevertheless to leave my mark on the project, for example by taking responsibility for the "loose ends" that other people left undone, with questions such as: who is going to organise this meeting, how is it that we all have doubts before we have even started, or what are your thoughts now about the composition of our group?

The mood in which we look back on this project is very typical of many organisation change projects: as a personal encounter, a shared adventure, a bit messy, with powerful and shared intentions and interventions, but also with uncertainties, disappointments and the question, what exactly was the point of all this . . . ?

The client's final words are an apt warning, which points out that my intrinsic responsibility has run away with me again. He writes: "I find your story a charming characterisation and a calm summary of the process and the project. In my view you are selling yourself short. Don't you set your aims ('permanent change in important values, convictions and ways of working') a bit too high? As a client that is not always what I expect of a consultant."

While his own responsibility decreases, the consultant must increasingly deal with himself and his own emotions. He attempts to find a new way of relating to the increasingly autonomous client. It is here that the consultant prematurely loses the assignment, the client and the success story. For me, this is often difficult and even depressing: the feeling of no longer being needed, no longer being able to make a real difference, and once again having to go out to look for new assignments and challenges. I notice that it is in this phase that I am most confronted with myself, with my own most essential needs, such as needs for inclusion, certainty and recognition. I feel a temptation to start compensating by taking on new responsibilities, coming up with new suggestions or doing my utmost to secure a follow-up assignment. I often

experience this phase as the most instructive for myself, even though it is not always the easiest. Time after time, I find myself having to accept the same basic truths about my relationships with my clients:
1. My clients really do know what is best for themselves.
2. I am not irreplaceable and my clients can manage very well without my help.
3. How difficult it is to let go and actually accept the autonomous continuation of an initiative, especially if that continuation has a new, unanticipated side to it.

It is precisely when facts like these depress you that you realise how important responsibility is for a consultant. After these painful new insights, I often remember in this phase that, just as with "power" (see Chapter 6), a consultant can choose not to take on any "responsibility". He can *choose* to be a non-responsible (which is different from irresponsible! and certainly different from non-responsive!) consultant. As already mentioned, a consultant actually has very little extrinsic responsibility: consulting contracts generally contain only obligations in terms of the effort to be put in and no responsibility for the outcome. The consultant is therefore concerned primarily with Aristotle's "efficient cause", while the other responsibilities remain with the client. Even if a consultant is asked, for example, to suggest or work out a strategy (formal cause!) or to assess the output of a division (final cause!), the authorisation and the ownership of the consultant's work lie with the client. And then it becomes clear that, as Machiavelli would have it, the responsibility of the consultant falls entirely within the responsibility of the client, and even the quality of the consultant is largely determined by the quality of the client.[5] As we saw earlier with fearless speech (Chapter 2), irony (Chapter 4) and powerlessness (Chapter 6): the subtle difference – compared, respectively, with flattery, sarcasm, dependence and, in this chapter, irresponsible behaviour – lies in the *intention* of the consultant. A professional consultant is intrinsically highly motivated to support the client and so on the one hand takes on little formal responsibility, but on the other hand is

---

5 "Here is an infallible rule; a prince who is not himself wise cannot be well advised, unless he happens to put himself in the hands of one individual who looks after all his affairs and is an extremely shrewd man" (Machiavelli, ca. 1514, XXIII.4). Unless, that is, the consultant takes over from the manager, in which case he ceases to be a consultant!

always willing to support the client – from the vantage point of that free, literally non-responsible position.

The fact that the consultant is predominantly working from the sidelines during the consolidation does not mean that he can no longer apply any powerful interventions. It is indeed possible as a consultant to intervene powerfully without taking on responsibility. Eastern "Zen consultants", for example, are true masters of the art of creative and powerful intervening, without taking over the problem or trying to solve it. I take a number of examples from the anthology *Zen flesh, Zen bones* (Senzaki & Reps, 1957):

1. Complete acceptance and resignation

By reacting as laconically as possible, the consultant can remain a consultant, even if pressure is exerted on him to become involved. This often helps the client to take real responsibility himself. An example from my practice is a client who has recently decided to start working with another consultant, because I could not be present on the day of the management board meeting. I was baffled by this decision: after everything we had been through, he was "trading me in" just because I couldn't get away to be there on a particular day! However, I believe that I was sincere when, without a shred of irony, I wished the client good luck with the other consultant. Here are two Zen examples:

An example: is that so?

The Zen master Hakuin was praised by his neighbours as one living a pure life.

A beautiful Japanese girl whose parents owned a food store lived near him. Suddenly, without any warning, her parents discovered she was with child.

This made her parents very angry. She would not confess who the man was, but after much harassment at last named Hakuin. In great anger the parents went to the master. "Is that so?" was all he would say.

After the child was born it was brought to Hakuin. By this time he had lost his reputation, which did not trouble him, but he took very good care of the child. He obtained milk from his neighbours and everything else the little one needed.

A year later the girl-mother could stand it no longer. She told her parents the truth – that the real father of the child was a young man who worked in the fishmarket.

The mother and father of the girl at once went to Hakuin to ask his forgiveness, to apologize at length, and to get the child back again.

Hakuin was willing. In yielding the child, all he said was: "Is that so?"
(Story 3 from *101 Zen Stories*, in Senzaki & Reps, 1957)

An example: right and wrong

When Bankei held his week-long meditation retreats, pupils from many parts of Japan came to attend. During one of these gatherings a pupil was caught stealing. The matter was reported to Bankei with the request that the culprit be expelled. Bankei ignored the case.

Later the pupil was caught in a similar act, and again Bankei disregarded the matter. This angered the other pupils, who drew up a petition asking for the dismissal of the thief, stating that otherwise they would leave in a body.

When Bankei had read the petition he called everyone before him. "You are wise brothers," he told them. "You know what is right and what is not right. You may go somewhere else to study if you wish, but this poor brother does not even know right from wrong. Who will teach him if I do not? I am going to keep him here even if all the rest of you leave."

A torrent of tears cleansed the face of the brother who had stolen. All desire to steal had vanished.
(Story 45 from *101 Zen Stories*, in Senzaki & Reps, 1957)

2. Contrary thinking and absurdity
The consultant pursues the intervention that is in fact precluded by the question. In other words, the consultant attempts to bring out the underlying premise by not working in accordance with that premise. In so doing, he shows that the client's very question imposes restrictions on the client. This often helps the client to consider his own opinions and investigate the extent to which those opinions rule out different perspectives. An example from my own practice was the occasion on which I thanked a director, after a long monologue, for his summary of what was going on in his organisation. There was silence

for a moment, until the two other directors present burst out laughing: the monologue had had nothing to do with what other people in the organisation thought important! Of course, their uproarious laughter did not do much for my relationship with the first director . . . Here is a Zen example:

> **An example: Joshu's Zen**
>
> Joshu began the study of Zen when he was sixty years old and continued until he was eighty, when he realized Zen.
>
> He taught from the age of eighty until he was one hundred and twenty.
>
> A student once asked him: "If I haven't anything in my mind, what shall I do?"
>
> Joshu replied: "Throw it out."
>
> "But if I haven't anything, how can I throw it out?" continued the questioner.
>
> "Well," said Joshu, "then carry it out."
> (Story 41 from *101 Zen Stories*, in Senzaki & Reps, 1957)

3. Redefining
In an extreme act of irony (see also Chapter 4) the consultant can completely redefine the situation into its opposite. This often helps the client to consider whether an intended decision really is the right way forward. Examples from my practice are the redefining of a working situation into a learning situation, or the rechristening of a work activity as a simulation or game. In such cases I suggest that my clients leave everything the same, that they conduct exactly the same conversations, make the same proposals and take the same decisions – but that they only *pretend* that this is real. An intervention of this kind often creates a lot of space and freedom. Here is a Zen example:

> **An example: the moon cannot be stolen**
>
> Ryokan, a Zen master, lived the simplest kind of life in a little hut at the foot of a mountain. One evening a thief visited the hut only to discover that there was nothing in it to steal.

Ryokan returned and caught him. "You may have come a long way to visit me," he told the prowler, "and you should not return empty-handed. Please take my clothes as a gift."

The thief was bewildered. He took the clothes and slunk away.

Ryokan sat naked, watching the moon. "Poor fellow," he mused, "I wish I could give him this beautiful moon."
(Story 9 from *101 Zen Stories*, in Senzaki & Reps, 1957)

4. Stepping outside polarities: not contributing anything, but also not contributing nothing
In another extreme act of irony (see also Chapter 4) the consultant can translate a dilemma into a possibility of sharing with the client how hair-raising both polarities are. This often helps the client to achieve a creative breakthrough. An example from my practice: in career counselling we sometimes conclude at the end of the process that continuing in the old job is impossible, but finding the way to the "ideal job" is equally impossible. The counsellor tries to keep this impasse in the room as long as possible, waiting for the creative "discovery"[6] that never fails to appear . . . Here is a Zen example:

An example: the short staff of Shuzan

Shuzan held out his short staff and said, "If you call this a short staff, you oppose its reality. If you do not call it a short staff, you ignore the fact. Now what do you wish to call this?"
(Story 43 from *The gateless gate*, in Senzaki & Reps, 1957)

5. Giving the assignment back on the principle that the client already has what he is looking for
The consultant can sometimes explicitly leave the responsibility for the assignment entirely with the client. This often helps the client to become aware of his own strength and only to use the consultant if it is really necessary. An example from my practice is derived from entry conversations, where it often helps to at least consider, together with the client, the possibility that the client can do it all himself, without

---

6   For this kind of unsought discovery Horace Walpole coined the word *serendipity* in 1754, commenting on the Sri Lankan story *The three princes of Serendip* in which the three princes make many of these discoveries. See Merton & Barber (2003).

the consultant. Strangely enough, that often leads to a consulting assignment, reframed but with a role for the consultant after all . . . Here is a Zen example:

An example: open your own treasure house

Daiju visited the master Baso in China. Baso asked: "What do you seek?" "Enlightenment," replied Daiju.

"You have your own treasure house. Why do you search outside?" Baso asked.

Daiju inquired: "Where is my treasure house?"

Baso answered: "What you are asking is your treasure house."

Daiju was enlightened! Ever after he urged his friends: "Open your own treasure house and use those treasures."
(Story 28 from *101 Zen Stories*, in Senzaki & Reps, 1957)

Conclusion

In the consolidation phase the art is to work without responsibility, but with great compassion, in other words with involvement, but without seeking to influence.

Interventions which are less appropriate for consolidating:
• Personal opinions;
• Suggestions, advice, new perspectives;
• Insistent fearless speech.

Interventions which are often more appropriate for consolidating:
• Naive questions;
• Supporting, helping actions;
• Contrary thinking and redefining;
• Increasing autonomy by explicitly giving back (parts of) the assignment.

We can imagine non-responsibility at the mid-point of a sliding scale with "non-responsive" and the "taking on of responsibilities" at either end. The consultant attempts to achieve mastery by staying away from these extremes and feeling comfortable in the middle zone, applying non-responsible consulting in a variety of situations.

Summary: consolidating and responsibility

Consolidating a consulting intervention amounts to **facilitating** the **responsibility** of the other person. During facilitating, consultant and client are therefore confronted predominantly with the various responsibilities that they bear:
1. The consultant makes sure that the client is looking after himself.
2. The client bears full responsibility for the outcome of the consulting process.

Extrinsic responsibility for the achievement of results in organisations can be broken down into four **areas of responsibility**:
1. Responsibility for the **input**, i.e. for the necessary materials and capacity ("material cause");
2. Responsibility for the **strategy**, i.e. for the design and planning ("formal cause");
3. Responsibility for the **task**, i.e. for the necessary work and initiatives ("efficient cause");
4. Responsibility for the **output**, i.e. for the final result ("final cause").

Conflicts in extrinsic responsibilities may arise in the case of:
- responsibility without mandate: lack of opportunity to influence one's own terms of reference;
- responsibility without materials: lack of opportunity to influence one's own suppliers;
- mandate without responsibility: lack of accountability, i.e. not being held accountable for one's own output.

Intrinsic responsibility refers to our personal readiness to bear responsibility, i.e. with **dedication**.

In consulting assignments, extrinsic responsibility gradually declines. Sometimes the consultant can even, in a constructive manner, adopt a **non-responsible** approach, by taking no extrinsic responsibility but remaining involved and dedicated intrinsically.

9
Characteristics of Departure and Letting Go

In the fifth phase of consulting, the phase of evaluation and departure, the consultant's aim is mainly to *end the consulting relationship in such a way that it can be rekindled whenever required*. The consultant is focused on letting go and stepping out of the client organisation, but then in a way that does not prevent further strengthening of the changes brought about by the consulting process.

In the theatre the boundaries are clear. We know when the play is over, if only because the lights go up and people around us start clapping and shuffling towards the exits. We have not really allowed the actors to become part of our life; we have only to walk out of the theatre to leave the whole plot behind us. Not so in consulting. In consulting, there is a strong investment by both client and consultant in the consulting relationship, and there are good reasons for continuing this relationship, even towards the end of the relationship. The client has the luxury of a knowledgeable and professional outsider, and the consultant has a steady income and feeling of being of service. So consultant and client can easily become mutually dependent on one another for their success and their survival. However, a productive consulting relationship stops, in my view, where dependence begins, just as giving advice stops where flattery begins and exploration stops where sarcasm begins (see Chapters 2 and 4).

At the start of the final phase of consulting the actual drama is over: the die has been cast and the client has made his choice. If all has gone well, the client can now call upon his new and unsuspected resources and steer a steady course through the turbulent waters surrounding him. The client monitors the changes independently and can begin reaping the benefits of those changes. Difficulties will arise where it is not clear that those benefits belong to the client and the client alone. There is a huge risk of excessive mutual dependence in this phase. On the one hand, with a successful outcome: who would want

to end a successful consulting process? The relationship is strong, consultant and client have achieved a lot together, they feel fulfilled. On
the other hand: where the results are unsatisfactory, the most obvious
thing is to point the finger of blame at the consultant, to recall him
and demand that he take action until the situation meets the client's
expectations. In both cases, there is an enormous risk that the discussions between client and consultant will drag on pointlessly. Although
he may be tempted to stay, the consultant is nevertheless responsible
for wrapping things up well in this phase. A good final evaluation
during the departure can help: expectations and risks are reviewed
systematically one more time, and the client is left with a document
which will enable him to continue monitoring the process himself.

As said before, it is important for both client and consultant to let go
and move on to more autonomous positions. Consulting is temporary
and bounded by clear limits of effectiveness, which can range from a
few minutes to a few years depending on the issues involved. Unless a
complete redefining and re-contracting of the assignment takes place,
a consultant who stays on for more than "enough time" usually just
gets in the way, or gradually changes his role from "consultant" to
"manager". Roger Harrison has taken issue with such mutual dependence and argued in favour of actively practising letting go. In his article
on organisations' addictions to consultants and their consultants'
co-dependency with organisations, he suggests a "cure" involving six
activities for consultants who want to "kick the habit" and help the
other person to do the same (Harrison, 1997):

1. First and foremost, we as consultants practise detachment. We let
   go of worry about situations in the client organisation and do not
   attempt to control what happens there. We abandon any personal
   mission to teach the client to live better. We do not depend on our
   clients emotionally or financially.
2. We approach our clients with integrity and with compassion,
   neither propagating our own version of the truth, nor distorting our
   truth to make it more palatable to our clients.
3. We let go of responsibility for any harm that our client organisations may do in the world, and for undoing or preventing it, except
   through speaking fearlessly. Neither do we take credit for the good
   they do, nor for the progress they make.
4. We acknowledge our own faults, inadequacies and betrayals to
   ourselves and to others, and to the best of our ability forgive those
   of our clients.

5. We seek to experience to the full any sorrow and despair which we feel over what is going on in our clients' organisations, so that we can be free of the apathy, powerlessness and emotional deadness that attend the suppression of these feelings.
6. While accepting the disturbing knowledge that many things are in a mess and we cannot fix all of them, we as consultants continue, with or without hope, to act in ways we believe are constructive.

The consultant who is able to let go will remain calm and attentive even in the most dramatic situations. She continues to work constructively in the client's interests, even where the situation threatens to put her off balance.

In order to support these quite solemn-sounding recommendations, the consultant can undertake some more practical and commonplace activities in this final stage of the consulting process, such as looking back with the client and evaluating the consulting process in order to formulate learning that can help with future assignments. Clients and consultants can also "celebrate" the end of the consulting assignment and thereby inform other interested parties of its termination.

In the following chapter I want to look at the position of the consultant who is no longer directly involved in the client's process. What interventions does a consultant who has literally become an outsider contribute? And how can we as consultants become "sadder but wiser" after every completed assignment, without succumbing to pessimism or cynicism?

♫

Summary: characteristics of departure and letting go

Consulting is a temporary collaborative relationship between client and consultant, the objective of which is an improvement in the client's fortunes.

Consulting is also an attitude or state of mind on the part of the consultant, which takes the following forms:
1. **Fearless speech**: open and honest, without fear of the consequences;
2. **Exploration**: listening to and interpreting what the client introduces;
3. **Self-monitoring and self-directing**: the ability to examine and direct the consulting activity itself from a different, sometimes more objective, perspective;
4. **Facilitating change**: being present during change, respecting the autonomous nature of change;
5. **Letting go** of what belongs to the client, practising detachment *vis-à-vis* the change that, as a consultant, one has become personally involved in.

In the fifth phase, that of **departure and evaluation**, the art of consulting appears to consist primarily of having the courage to let go and to give the client full credit for the success or failure of the assignment.

Six activities that are appropriate in **letting go**:
1. Freeing oneself of the urge to teach the client something and to be emotionally or financially dependent on the client;
2. Continuing to speak fearlessly with integrity and compassion, without distorting or propagating one's own truth;
3. Not taking responsibility for positive or negative effects of the assignment;
4. Forgiving one's own faults, shortcomings and inadequacies, and those of the client;
5. Contemplating one's own disappointments and disillusionment, and not allowing oneself to be bound by the powerlessness and paralysis that are sometimes the result of such emotions;
6. Accepting that many things are not as they should be and that we cannot fix them – and nevertheless continuing to be constructive.

Three activities that are appropriate in **saying goodbye and evaluating**:
1. Celebrating the completed assignment;
2. Jointly drawing conclusions and lessons;
3. Formally evaluating (the effects of) the consulting process.

10
Letting Go and Tragic Consulting

I want to learn more and more to see as beautiful what is necessary in things;
then I shall be one of those who make things beautiful.
Amor fati: *let that be my love henceforth!*
(Nietzsche, *The Gay Science*, 1882)

Man's greatness lies in his capacity to recognise his wretchedness.
(Pascal, *Pensées*, 1670)

The consultant as committed outsider

In letting go and stepping out of the consulting process, the consultant, together with the client, reviews what has been done, and what has been achieved. The consultant returns to being a complete outsider, uninvolved and non-responsible. In the ideal case this transition is relaxed and almost imperceptible because the consultant has been able to remain a fearless, non-responsible outsider during the consulting process itself. Taking leave then makes hardly any difference in the relationship.

I find that letting go is not always that easy. I have therefore made it a habit to "put the end at the beginning": I consciously try to begin new assignments by letting go. Then I observe my own impatience, fascination, motivation, affinity or whatever emotion arises – and notice that they are less of an obstacle the more I pay attention to them.

Actually, there are a lot of consultants for whom letting go is not as easy as it sounds. The consultant invests in the assignment and in the consulting relationship, and has often given generously of his own "intrinsic" responsibility (see Chapter 8). In addition, the consultant cannot avoid nursing all sorts of expectations in relation to the future and all sorts of notions of "what is best for the client". Letting go of the consulting process therefore often requires great effort. In addition, senior consultants often impress upon their younger colleagues that it is best *not* to let go of an assignment, as experience is seen as a great asset in the world of consulting. Usually, the assignments they carry around constitute the consultant's experience. And if experience has a positive connotation with consultants, they tend to carry a lot about with them. That may only make it more difficult to process that experience, to learn from it what there is to be learned, and then to let go.

Letting go has to do with one's relationship to one's own experiences and starts with being able to examine those experiences, including everything that was *not* successful and all of the aspirations that were *not* fulfilled. This can be particularly difficult in the event of stagnating change or of assignments that take a "fatal" turn, for example due to situational irony (see Chapter 4). As a result, consultants have developed defences against really letting go.

In my experience, a consultant must slowly "sweat out" every assignment, gradually allowing it to settle down in his own experience. In this chapter I intend to look at whether and how this can be done in the case of the most powerful experiences, the real *tragedies* of the consultant, in order to determine which attitudes and intentions are most conducive to consulting.

A consultant at work

An e-mail interview with Roger Harrison, organisation development consultant and writer:

How was it for you to let go of the profession of consultant?
It was difficult in the extreme to let go of my profession. I had strongly identified with my work and in leaving it and at the same time moving to another part of the country, I went from being a well known and respected professional to being "no one".

As a child I had been awkward and bookish, and I had come to believe that my only positive contribution was through my intellect. As an adult I came to believe that the main reason people might want me around was if I was able to help them solve problems. Now I wasn't solving people's problems any more.

I had also been raised to believe that if one is not economically productive, one scarcely deserves to live. For all these reasons I found retirement damaging to my self esteem. I felt isolated and useless, and I experienced a great deal of depression for several years. The story of how I came out of that depression is the story of how I came to feel that I was worthwhile to others without "doing".

Consultants are often "outsiders" or "bystanders". Have you become more of an "insider" now you have left the profession?
I am more of an insider. For the first time, I feel myself to be a valued and integrated member of the community in which I live. That was not true in any previous community, including my community of origin.

Nietzsche speaks about "amor fati": to love your fate, suggesting that co-dependency can also be counterbalanced by "rapture" and "embracing", rather than "letting go". What would you say to that idea?
I have never been very prone to rapture myself as I am naturally detached. I find it hard to get swept away by emotions. When I wrote the article about "letting go" (Harrison, 1997), I was thinking more of letting go of my own passions and agendas than of those of my clients. Nietzsche's idea seems like a life-affirming choice and also a dangerous one, as it seems to lead to being increasingly overwhelmed and intoxicated. However, what would Nietzsche say to the response that there is already so much grief in our lives – why take on the grief of someone else as well?

What would you do differently now when you are asked for consultation?
I am much more likely to offer my presence and my heart, and less likely to offer advice.

The chorus in Greek tragedy

In his first book, philologist and classicist Friedrich Nietzsche (1872) examines in depth the origins of tragedy, the very first, "historical" origins of tragedy in ancient Greece as well as the sources of any tragedy at the very moment of its inception. The book provides new answers to the question that has preoccupied thinkers since the time of Aristotle: *why does tragedy give pleasure?*[1] I intend to follow Nietzsche's analysis closely here, because he provides a new perspective on the role of the consultant that has received insufficient attention so far in this book as well as in other books on consulting.

A reflection: the Dionysian and Apollonian in our culture

Nietzsche (1872) distinguishes two main "undercurrents" in Western culture that come to expression in works of art and other forms of production:

---

1   For a more recent discussion of this question, see the book *Why does tragedy give pleasure?* by Nuttall (1996).

- The *Apollonian* is the ability to create images, structures and dreams. It lies at the basis of technical accomplishments, epic poetry and prose, glamorous illusions, complex organisations and ambitious visions. Nietzsche finds a metaphor for these creative abilities in the Greek god of light Apollo, the god of truth-telling, moderation and self-knowledge.
- The *Dionysian* is the ability to create enchantment and rapture in music. It lies at the basis of uninhibited creativity, of lyricism, connectedness and passions. Nietzsche finds a metaphor for these creative abilities in the obscure Greek god Dionysus, who is said to have brought wine and rapture to Greece.

The Apollonian creates from nature, while the Dionysian becomes submerged in nature. According to Nietzsche both undercurrents played a role in the development of Greek tragedy, which was enacted every year as a "satyr-song" or "goat-song"[2] on the feast days of Dionysus. Nietzsche states that after the period of the tragedies, since Socrates Western culture made many attempts to suppress the "dangerous", "irrational" Dionysian element in creative endeavours. He would probably recognise this even today in strikingly one-sided Apollonian creations such as multinational enterprises and high-quality products and in the marginalisation of Dionysian escapism and (religious, spiritual, drug-induced) rapture. But he would also acknowledge that no single society has ever succeeded in banishing the Dionysian completely, simply because it is one of the human life forces.

According to Nietzsche, the classical tragedy is a unique art form, because it is the only one that manages to reconcile two opposing inspirations, Apollonian and Dionysian.

In order to offer a new answer to the age-old question of what pleasure tragedy gives, Nietzsche first refers back to the origins of tragedy, during the mystery plays dedicated to the god Dionysus. In that oldest form, tragedy was devoted to the *suffering* of Dionysus: how he was cut into pieces by the Titans in his youth, and how, immortal as he was, he lived on in that condition, as a horribly mutilated demon yet at the same time a kind and generous ruler. It is said that the gods of Olympus sprang from his laughter and the whole human race from his tears. In the oldest tragedies, according to Nietzsche, a notion of a healed and restored unity was expressed. On the stage there was only the chorus

---

2 "Goat-song" is the literal translation of the Greek word *tragoedia*.

of goat-like satyrs, singing and dancing in a state of rapture. In the works of the tragedian Thespis, at some point the leader of the chorus steps forth and becomes the protagonist. Aeschylus increased the number of actors from one to two and Sophocles to three (Aristotle, *Poetica*, 4th century BC).

An example

A City stockbroking firm plans to introduce a new IT system within the next few months, to replace the old system on which the actual trading has been done for over 20 years. In recent years there have already been four organisation-wide attempts to replace the antiquated system. All of those attempts have failed, mainly due to suspicion and inertia on the part of the London brokers. The management team realises that it will be no easier this time: the new system will not work perfectly right away and will entail many more disadvantages than advantages for the users in the short term. How to motivate people under these circumstances? From the very outset we, as consultants, come up against deeply ingrained convictions ("You motivate people with money, with extra bonuses!") and a stubborn cynicism ("Sure enough, we've been making a loss for years and always will do. But head office cannot afford to shut down the London branch, so we're sitting pretty."). We decide to explore more extensively with the help of individual interviews and at the same time to set up dialogue groups so that staff have a platform to help prepare themselves for the coming changes. The interviews are often dramatic. The conversation with the IT project leader, for example, lasts over three hours and is an endless, despondent account of opposition and discrimination. Other staff members report that the scapegoats for the failure of the IT implementation are already being identified and that the project leader is at the top of the hit list. Our dialogue groups are always organised around copious lunches ("In order to motivate people to turn up!") but nevertheless face low turnouts. Those who do take part tell us that they don't expect "this" (the consulting process) to last more than a month nor to have any impact whatsoever. We also experience what it is like to be the target of discrimination, for example when participants in the dialogues make indirect comments about the "general decline in the quality of the English language". Within a month, all of the cynical predictions of our counterparts come true: the IT implementation is experiencing huge delays, dialogue groups are being cancelled and, after a change in the management team, our calls are no longer being returned. Our time in this firm has made us gloomy. During our whole stay we felt "doomed" in a way, as if certain defeat is close at hand but time has been postponed at the last minute. We noticed all around us a tragic lack of motivation coupled with an

equally tragic co-dependence, as a result of which the lack of motivation
does not lead to any action or change. We find ourselves mere witnesses
to the events, but also unwanted and powerless to do anything about
them . . .

The importance of the chorus can also be seen in the titles of the Greek
tragedies: nine of the 31 surviving tragedies are named after the chorus
(leaving only around two-thirds named after the protagonist). There
are very different ways in which the choruses relate to the action:
sometimes they give a moral judgement, sometimes they bemoan the
fate of the hero, sometimes they attempt to influence leading actors to
refrain from intended actions, sometimes they act as a sort of midwife
to decisions and actions, and sometimes they wrestle with their own
urges to take action. There seem to be at least as many chorus roles as
consulting roles (see Chapter 5). But the two most salient characteristics in my view, which are found in all choruses, are "honest naivety"
and "involvement with the other person".

It is interesting in this connection that many of the Greek tragedies
are not in fact tragedies but "reconciliation dramas" in which the
protagonist comes to terms with his or her unpalatable fate. In these
plays the conflicts and passions of the protagonists slowly fade into the
background, to make way for an escape, reconciliation and *letting go* of
those conflicts and passions. Sometimes this is the third part of a trilogy
and, often, the city of Athens is symbolically the place where the
reconciliation occurs. In these dramas, the protagonists are followed
in the final stages of their significant transitions, so they actually take
place *after* the real action is over. Examples of reconciliation dramas
are *The Persians* and *Eumenides* by Aeschylus (5th century BC),
Philoctetes and *Oedipus at Colonus* by Sophocles (5th century BC) and
Alcestis, *Helen* and *Iphigenia in Tauris* by Euripides (5th century BC).

If the tragedy evolved from the chorus, the question is: what is the
significance of the chorus? What purpose do the members of the chorus
serve in the representation of the drama? Nietzsche starts with a
summary of previous answers to this question:
1. Aristotle (4th century BC) tells us in *The Athenian Constitution*
   (Chapter 56) that the members of the chorus were chosen from
   well-to-do Athenian citizens, and suggests that members of the
   chorus should be seen as representatives of political figures.

2. Schiller (1803), in his preface to *The Bride of Messina*,[3] describes the chorus as "a living wall which tragedy erects around itself in order to close itself off entirely from the real world, and to maintain for itself its ideal ground and its poetic freedom".
3. According to Schlegel (1809), the chorus always expresses the playwright's thoughts about the action and acts as an ideal onlooker who enables the real onlooker to face his own feelings about the horrifying drama in a more gentle and poetic form. The chorus therefore gives expression to what the public "should think" at any point in the drama.

Nietzsche agrees most with Schiller's answer, but goes a step further. He claims that the chorus is the representative and expression of that uninhibited natural state which is so often threatened by ordering and structuring tendencies. The chorus should therefore be regarded as a citizen who has completely forgotten his civil status and responsibilities and has been transformed, as it were, into an original state like that of a newborn baby: universal, timeless and imperturbable. Nietzsche describes the chorus as a Dionysian rapture that allows itself to be enchanted by Apollonian stories and images (see "A reflection: the Dionysian and Apollonian in our culture", above).

Both Schiller and Nietzsche convey the idea of the chorus as a protective and uninhibited witness that remains present in the drama, encompasses the drama and allows it to develop further in a natural manner. The chorus is therefore, according to Nietzsche, also a fearless speaker, an *ungeschminkter Ausdruck der Wahrheit* (unvarnished expression of truth). The chorus is thus not merely a spectator, as Aristotle and Schlegel suggest, but an *examiner* of the drama, a participant who experiences the drama personally.

It is interesting to watch a Greek tragedy with this hypothesis in mind and to see how the chorus responds to the action. In the surviving tragedies, those of Aeschylus, Sophocles and Euripides, the chorus is never the protagonist, not even if the tragedy is named after the chorus. The chorus has no freedom of action in terms of its own needs and desires.

---

3   In this tragedy Schiller attempts to recreate the Greek tragedy with chorus as authentically as possible.

Often, the chorus is a flat character to such an extent that it can figure as a pure and clean "sounding board" for the desires, fears and doubts of the protagonists. It takes many forms: "advisers at the Persian court", "women of Thebes", "slaves of Athens", "old men of Argos" or "onlookers drawn by morbid fascination" (in *Iphigenia in Aulis* by Euripides, 5th century BC). Generally, the participants in the chorus represent less powerful members of the depicted society. The chorus consists of directly involved onlookers who are ensnared by the drama and give expression to the anxieties, beliefs and uncertainties that the drama stirs up within them, but without being able to intervene.

The tragic consultant

In my view, the tragic chorus as described above is a marvellous image of the consultant at his best, namely the timeless, imperturbable consultant in the final phase of a consulting process. In their description of the function of the chorus in Greek tragedy, Schiller and Nietzsche provide a sort of "paragon" for many consultants in business organisations: the consultant who has the appropriate *intention* in each and every tragedy. This does not mean that the chorus in Greek tragedies are always successful or heroic consultants. On the contrary, it is precisely their struggles and failures that are striking and recognisable. However, they do almost always have the right motivation and intention in consulting. The parallel between consultant and tragic chorus contains all sorts of recognisable elements. The consultant and chorus can both be described as:

- a "garment" that provides the protagonists/clients with dignity and tranquillity, and makes the form of these protagonists/clients "recognizable rather than bearing them down with heaviness" (Schiller, 1803);
- "persistent witness and sustainer of the action" (Schiller, 1803);
- the person who changes the perspective from the "inner circle of the action to broaden it into the past, the future, distant times and peoples, and the 'human condition'" (Schiller, 1803);
- the person who "countenances the upset of passions to forge a transition from these emotions to quiet meditation", by "unpicking diverse aspects" and "liberating reflection from action" (Schiller, 1803);
- the person who verbalizes the unpleasant or painful, so that it can be examined and then, possibly, processed;
- the person who introduces new perspectives into the entangled inner world of the protagonist;

- the person who sympathises and becomes enraptured, even while retaining his own detachment as an outsider;
- the person who, due to the nature of his own role, cannot really intervene in the actions of the protagonists/clients, although he often has that illusion and that inclination;
- the person who can bring about a reconciliation between the Apollonian (objective, individualising, enterprising) and the Dionysian (personal, connecting, contemplative).

The Greek tragedy that has been handed down to us can be viewed as a consulting process on many levels. In the first place, the annual performances during the feasts of Dionysus were long "consulting conversations" with the rulers and the *dhemos* (public assembly) of Athens. The tragedians were deservedly called the teachers and advisers of the people of Athens, as Aristophanes emphasises at various points in his *Frogs* (405 BC). Throughout the Golden Age of Athens, from the Battle of Salamis in 480 BC to the final and complete defeat and capture by Sparta in 404 BC, the leaders of the city attended performances of the works of the great tragedians: from the oldest surviving tragedy, *The Persians* from 472 BC, to the newest, *Oedipus in Colonus*, written by Sophocles probably shortly before his death in 405 BC.

But consulting also has an important place *within* the tragedies: prophets, messengers and gods play consulting roles in each of the surviving tragedies. In addition, the protagonists advise each other regularly. However, within this wealth of consulting, the consulting role of the chorus remains unique: the chorus is often passive, has a relatively modest position and rank, never moves from its spot. Over all, the chorus is an intimately connected but rather powerless consultant, which is just how today consultants often feel with their clients. But no consultant I know is so intimately connected and at the same time so capable of retaining an independent perspective as the chorus in most tragedies.[4]

---

4 And sometimes this "retaining of perspective" proves to be a thankless task, as the chorus found in *Iphigenia in Tauris* (Euripides, 5th century BC), when the protagonists decided to sacrifice it cruelly in order to secure their own escape. They were perhaps the first, but not the last, consultants to discover how an assignment is sometimes completed successfully at the cost of the relationship with the consultant or even damage to the consultant's reputation.

A reflection: personality differences between consultants and managers

There are more and more indications that consultants and managers often have complementary personalities. Magerison & Lewis (1980) point out a clear complementarity between consultants and managers in terms of the most widely used and best documented personality typology, the *Myers-Briggs Type Indicator* (MBTI). The population of managers appears to peak in the dimensions S, T and J, while consultant populations peak around the opposing dimensions N, F and P. Managers therefore tend towards concrete observation, thinking and controlling, while consultants tend towards developing intuition, feeling and letting go.

The variable for expressing differences between populations is the *self-selection ratio (SSR)*, the ratio between the occurrence of preferences in those populations compared with the average profile. An SSR of 2 for a particular group and a particular Myers-Briggs type means that that group has *twice* as many individuals of that type as the general population. For the Ashridge Business School, the distribution of its clients' MBTIs peaks around ESTJ (SSR: 2.0) and ISTJ (SSR: 1.04) [Carr *et al.* 2005]. The distribution of the *Ashridge faculty* peaks around the exactly complementary fields of INFP (SSR: 5.3) and ENFP (SSR: 3.6) – when comparing both populations with the total population of the United Kingdom.[5] In the largest database I was able to find, that of Macdaid *et al.* (1986), with a worldwide population of as many as 232 557 MBTI profiles, the highest SSRs for the 7463 managers occur around ESTJ (SSR: 1.86) and ENTJ (SSR: 2.00), and for the 1803 counsellors around INFP (SSR: 1.57). The SSRs are indeed a bit lower, probably because the averaging took place over a much wider diversity. This complementarity can be compared with that pointed out by Nietzsche between the Apollonian and the Dionysian. The STJ profile certainly has Apollonian traits: according to the MBTI handbook (Briggs Myers *et al.*, 1998), these types are practical, matter-of-fact, realistic and logical decision-makers. Their orderly, constructive, practical, organised and theorising nature is something they share with Apollonian art. The NFP profile, on the other hand, has undeniably Dionysian characteristics: according to the MBTI handbook, these "types" are enthusiastic, insightful, flexible and adaptable innovators. Their openness, lack of inhibition and improvisation are features they have in common with Dionysian art.

---

5   Judy Curd, personal communication.

After all of these analogies between chorus and consultant, it is interesting to see how the chorus is closely involved in the action, but at the same time lets go of it and does not influence the events in general. The task of the chorus is to reflect on the action in a detached yet emotionally involved manner, not to be a protagonist of that action. Most choruses, as adviser to the protagonist, appear to opt for a coach role (see Chapter 5).

According to Nietzsche, the chorus is "a surrender of the individual through an entering into an unfamiliar nature. And indeed this phenomenon emerged in epidemic proportions; a whole crowd felt itself enchanted in this way (. . .). The dithyrambic chorus is a chorus of people who have been transformed, who have completely forgotten their past as citizens, their social position: they have become the timeless servants of their god, living outside all spheres of society."[6] I cannot deny that I sometimes have a similar feeling as a consultant.

Nietzsche is also saying something here about the collaboration between different consultants and the ease with which those consultants, "in their Dionysian intoxication", begin to think and feel the same way about the client and the client organisation. This is a (transference) phenomenon that has always struck me as extraordinarily powerful: when two or more different consultants start work within the same client organisation or collaborate on the same assignment, they quickly start to feel the same and confirm each other in their behaviour with respect to the client. The same phenomenon is also observed in the consulting of consultants, i.e. in *shadow consulting*[7] (Schroder, 1974): countertransference appears to be quite contagious.

---

6   Nietzsche (1872; § 8). It sounds even better in German: "*Hier ist bereits ein Aufgeben des Individuums durch Einkehr in eine fremde Natur. Und zwar tritt dieses Phänomen epidemisch auf: eine ganze Schar fühlt sich in dieser Weise verzaubert (. . .) der dithyrambische Chor ist ein Chor von Verwandelten, bei denen ihre bürgerliche Vergangenheit, ihre soziale Stellung völlig vergessen ist: sie sind die zeitlosen, außerhalb die Gesellschaftssphären lebenden Diener ihres Gottes geworden.*"

7   Although it is also possible that shadow consultants may unconsciously display *inverse* behaviour compared with that of the consultant(s), and therefore start to behave in some respects like the client in the original consulting process (see Chapter 11 of De Haan, 2004b). Perhaps there is something similar going on in the extended example of shadow consulting in the Epilogue to this book.

A reflection: transference

In the relationship between client and consultant, things happen that also happen between the client and others and between the consultant and others. With the consultant, the client repeats patterns of interaction that he has already experienced with other people, patterns of interaction that may shed some light on the client's problem. This phenomenon of repetition of patterns that originate outside the consulting situation itself is what Freud called *transference* (*Übertragung* – see Freud, 1912a) or, more specifically, *transference* when it occurs in the client and *countertransference* when it occurs in the consultant. Transference is often recognised as responses, in yourself or in the client, that appear disproportionate or have little to do with what has just been said. It is worthwhile for the consultant to unravel carefully – and sometimes with the client – "what" belongs to "whom", i.e.: "What originates within myself?" and "What does the other person trigger in me?"

When we watch a Greek tragedy and allow ourselves to become "enraptured" by it, we are in fact taking part in shadow consulting. We generally identify most readily with the chorus. In the comments of the members of the chorus, who often express hope, complaints, fears and uncertainties about the future, we can best recognise ourselves. We frequently find[8] that the chorus puts into words our own anxieties and our own polarised emotions (hope and fear!) for the future. For us as consultants, it is therefore easy to answer Nietzsche's initial question: *what pleasure does a Greek tragedy give?* For us, a tragedy is a unique consulting situation that we can observe without having to intervene, and without bearing responsibility for the outcome:

• We have a client (the protagonist) who, together with a number of other interested parties (fellow actors), comprise a client organisation in which important issues are being dealt with.
• We observe consultants at work (the chorus), and see how they become enraptured and deepen their connection with the client.

---

8   Like Schlegel (1809), as is clear from the significance that he attributes to the chorus.

- And, finally, we observe ourselves, as shadow consultant to the consultants, with emotions that are often parallel or opposite to those of the consultants, inspired by our countertransference.

The pleasure therefore lies in experiencing a safe consulting situation, where we do not have to do anything and so cannot do anything wrong.

I cannot emphasise strongly enough the vital role of *countertransference* in consulting: what we recognise in our client are our *own* emotions, our *own* hope and fear for the future, and our *own* struggles. Via that recognition we often get stuck in our consulting practice in a clichéd response, which we carry with us from client to client. When we watch a tragedy we can witness how this also happens to other consultants, namely how dramatic issues and situations involving the protagonists produce typical response patterns in the members of the chorus, such as:[9]
- giving voice to the haunting unconscious of the protagonist (in *Eumenides*);
- generating deeper insight by exploring what the protagonist experiences and interpreting his words and actions (in *Prometheus*);
- coaching the protagonist actively to accept his own destiny (in *Alcestis*);
- continuing with constructive and helping behaviour even where they are constantly treated with contempt by the protagonists (in *Iphigenia in Tauris*);
- trying to intervene but staying always one step behind the unfolding events (in *Ajax*);
- drawing a veil over increasingly horrific events (for example, in *Medea* or *Hippolytus*);

---

9   The examples have been chosen from the few tragedies that have survived in full: seven by Aeschylus, seven by Sophocles, and 17 by Euripides. *Eumenides* and *Prometheus* are by Aeschylus (5th century BC), *Ajax* and *Antigone* are by Sophocles (5th century BC), and *Alcestis, The Bacchae, Hecuba, Hippolytus, Iphigenia in Tauris, Medea* and *Orestes* are by Euripides (5th century BC).

- becoming so engrossed in their own destiny that they remain available to the protagonist only with extreme difficulty (in *Hecuba*);
- becoming completely absorbed in Dionysian intoxication and enchantment (in *The Bacchae*);
- giving themselves over to moral indignation that increases and leaves virtually no doubt (in *Antigone*);
- being led astray by naivety and goodwill to explain away the deeds of and even support wrong-doers (in *Orestes*, one of the bleakest surviving tragedies).

We then notice in ourselves how preferential inclinations develop: the inclination to help, to want to warn the protagonist, not being able to contain ourselves, being angry or disappointed with our clients, etc.

I define a tragic consultant as a person who does not indulge in the above and remains present as a helping *outsider*, even in dramatic situations, and is aware of the partly tragic and ineluctable nature of those situations.

This tragic consultant must ask himself in the first instance why he actually became a consultant. What was it in his own biography that compelled him to become a consultant in the first place and then to continue in that role? It then often becomes clear that the consultant's parents and other family members appealed strongly to his consulting qualities and put him in a particular position of "helpfulness" within the family. I myself identify with this: due to unique circumstances in my own youth, I ultimately chose a profession that is new and unusual in my own family, after first following a more obvious course of study (physics) where I did not feel at home.

The helpful outsider therefore practised the role of helpful outsider even at an early stage, namely within his own family. The later decision to choose the profession of helpful outsider is based on a dual motivation: to help others on the one hand, and (thereby) to help oneself on the other. That decision is often strongly influenced by the desire to "put right" something that previously went wrong, for example poor advising or not so helpful behaviour on the part of the parents, associated with the parents' tendency to behave like a "client" and (mis)use children to fulfil their own emotional needs.

The tragic consultant: when it comes to real problems and situations where various options have already been tried out, client and consultant reflect together on tragic undercurrents – and they often play out these tragic undercurrents unawares, with a "chorus" of internalised consultants in the background.

This desire to put right experiences from the past has extraordinarily positive consequences for the helping professional. It results in a great sensitivity to and genuine empathy with clients, and the ability to keep one's chin up, even in difficult circumstances. But it is also a threat to one's own effectiveness, namely where the same professional cannot let go of his own need "to atone" and becomes dependent on the whims of or the improvements in the client. Consulting then becomes a *self-assigned impossible task*. This impossible task is an outstanding example of the situational irony (see Chapter 4) of the consultant: the expert in the field of helping often turns out to have an underlying problem with his own neediness!

Vega Zagier Roberts (1994), who writes about this self-assigned impossible task, sees in the self-awareness of (organisations of) helping professionals an incentive to maintain a vicious circle. The professional starts consulting in order to sort himself out, meets with disappointment and then starts to consult more oppressively or even harder, resulting in further disappointment. Zagier Roberts also sees the effects of this process in the identity formation of many consulting organisations. The *identity* of an organisation has to do with its main function and what distinguishes it from other organisations that fulfil the same function. In the case of helping outsiders, this identity is often connected with their own ideals and ideology. Their own identity is therefore connected with their own intrinsic responsibility (see Chapter 8), which is often very strong, as is shown by the fact that consultants often tend to deliver more than is strictly described in the contract. Internal conversations in consultancies often focus on how exceptionally good and unique the consultancy is, while expressions of doubt and scepticism are met with rejection and even anxiety. The consultants reinforce their own ideology further by regarding the clients and customers as people who "still have a lot to learn" and by presenting themselves as healthy, wise and omniscient.

The only alternative to this vicious circle is a tragic attitude (see, for example, Unamuno, 1912), in which we acknowledge that we come into consulting with certain needs and thereby contaminate, distort and disrupt the consulting process from the outset. The tragic consultant pursues an understanding of his own, self-assigned impossible task and his own reasons for starting this work in the first place, and remains attentive to and alert for ways in which those needs may kick in, thereby making letting go impossible.

If the consultant is not able to understand his own needs throughout the consulting process, the consequences are often more negative than simply the inability to let go. All sorts of less conscious reactions may occur, such as:
• the projection of those needs and uncertainties onto others,
• the idealising of the consultant's contribution and
• going over the top in a helping role. (Zagier Roberts, 1994)

These may lead in turn to the perversion of the right intention that is so essential in consulting, so that flattery, manipulation or the taking on of unnecessary responsibilities may start to predominate. Instead of a tragic consultant, the helping outsider now becomes the protagonist himself, namely of the "tragedy of the person who lives from his helping" (Stroeken, 1988). He becomes enslaved by consulting and the need to keep proving himself as a consultant, and can accept himself only for a short time after receiving "positive feedback" from clients. The consultant must now satisfy his own desire to be helpful without ever being able to raise the subject, even though that is the main motive behind his helping activities. This *helper's syndrome* is described in many places in the literature, see, for example, Miller (1979) or Stroeken (1988). Interestingly enough, it is precisely his own *neediness* that has taken possession of the consultant in this syndrome, either openly and dominating, or split off and (as far as possible) removed from the conscious mind.[10]

An example

This consultancy is headed by four experienced consultants, each of which indulges his own helper's syndrome in their profession, i.e. with his clients and with the other consultants in the organisation. The most senior director is increasingly afraid of his clients. For example, he lies awake at night before the start of a new assignment or a new programme in which he is the main tutor. In order to control that fear, he has decided not to serve any more clients with a significantly higher level of education or a higher status than himself. Nevertheless, he still feels that he must always prove himself, and as a result has become very skilled at flattery. In addition, he invoices for over one and a half times the annual agreed turnover in terms of consulting days.

Things seem to be going quite well for the second director. He withdraws completely into the role of consultant, not only with his clients but also internally, within the organisation. He appoints himself as mentor to everyone else within the organisation and invites them to come to him, particularly to vent their worries.

He also enjoys reading and teaching the other consultants about the books that he has just read. However, sometimes this self-satisfaction and control suddenly break down. Then he is plagued by uncontrollable attacks of anger in which he abuses colleagues or goes around slamming doors. At the other extreme, when given a compliment, he can suddenly burst into tears and appear very moved.

The third director has two tried and tested recipes for eliminating the syndrome, albeit temporarily, from his mind: humour and beer. His passion for humour is sometimes at the expense of others, for example when he

---

10 As also pointed out in Chapter 4, this is the *situational irony* of many consultants.

makes up cruel nicknames for fellow consultants or his clients or cracks jokes about their weak spots. His great thirst for beer helps him to staunch regular outbursts of anger and attacks of anxiety.

The fourth consultant finds it difficult to stand his ground in this setting and often feels excluded by the other three, just as he felt excluded as a small child by the other children in the apartment building where he grew up. He keeps on trying to do his very best, to impress and, above all, not to make anyone angry. He comes up with new initiatives regularly and endlessly checks whether the others approve. However, this only results in his interpreting any word of criticism by clients or other consultants as a personal affront, which makes it even harder for him to maintain his position and makes him try even harder to impress.

Despite the obvious difference in their impact on consulting, there is often only a thin line separating tragic consulting and becoming submerged in one's own "consultant's tragedy". In tragic consulting, one contemplates the tragedy of one's own assignments and is aware of one's own motives and needs. And when submerged, one becomes the suffering subject of a tragedy that arises when a great help deficit on the part of the consultant is compensated by a great desire to be meaningful and helpful to others. The tragic consultant can only prevent his own tragedy from gaining the upper hand by means of regular and critical self-monitoring (see Chapter 5), preferably with the help of a shadow consultant or coach.

For a tragic consultant, his own attempt at self-monitoring starts with his own involvement in what is happening now. During the consulting process he is always conscious of a choice, between:
- on the one hand, becoming absorbed in and co-resonating with what the client brings, so becoming absorbed by one's own sensitivity and empathy; and
- on the other hand, observing one's own rapture and endeavouring to understand what is going on at any moment, and in whom it is going on.

The first option often leads to a strengthening of the rapture, in the consultant and also in the other person. It therefore leads to a suggestible and suggestive, "hypnotic" form of consulting and often to a powerful intervention in the client's situation. The other option leads in general to a more "analytical" approach in which letting go plays an important role at each moment in the consulting process.

A practical case: the five dramatic phases in a consultation group

In De Haan (2004a) I showed how consulting processes and tragedies also resemble each other in aspects such as "time boundedness" and "causality". There are clear similarities between the five phases proposed in the literature for consultants (see, for example, Bell & Nadler, 1979, or Kubr, 1996) and the five phases proposed in drama literature (see, for example, Bradley, 1904):

1. The entry phase resembles the phase of *exposition* in the drama.
2. The exploration phase resembles the phase of *development* in the drama.
3. The implementation phase resembles the phase of *crisis* and *peripeteia* in the drama.
4. The consolidation phase resembles the phase of *denouement* in the drama.
5. The evaluation phase resembles the phase of *catastrophe* and *exodus* in the drama.

Here is one example (one of many) of the tragic course of a consulting assignment. I am the process facilitator of a peer consultation group of managers at a large flower auction house. The *exposition* (phase 1!) took place years ago, and involved our getting to know all of the internal consultants in the organisation. We helped those internal consultants to develop their consulting skills. The *development* (phase 2!) consists of the launch of a number of peer consultation groups and *action learning* (see De Haan, 2004b) with consultants. The success of peer consultation groups gradually becomes better known within the organisation. Increasingly, not only consultants, but also managers get together for around one half-day a month to discuss tricky issues and situations in their organisation. While earlier groups continue without external facilitation, my colleagues and I are called in to set up new groups.

At their fourth consultation session, developments in one of the groups appear to be reaching an impasse. In two consecutive sessions, the group focuses on the same *people management case* of one of the managers, Fred, about the leadership of one of the project leaders, Lex. The group keeps coming to the same conclusions: confirming Fred's current approach, suggesting that he worry less and giving practical tips for further improvement. However, a month after the second session I receive an e-mail with a request to facilitate a discussion between Fred, his manager Piet and a consultant from Human Resources. After months of struggling, the case has come to a *crisis* (phase 3!) for Fred. Before attending the meeting, I review my notes from the consultation sessions. I wonder how such an apparently innocuous case can have escalated so far. The conversation at the auction house begins with Fred outlining his situation again, just as he has done twice before. Since he appears very frustrated at having to try again, we waste no time on additional questions and giving confirmation or feedback. We address Fred directly and ask him: "Why is it that you are making such a huge issue of this case? What does this actually say about your own *people management* style?"

The discussion lasts nearly three hours and ends emotionally when Fred discovers that he has never actually been responsible for this situation – that the leadership should come from Piet – but that he has taken it on himself in order to prove something to himself, in order to be a sort of white knight for the whole department. After this complete about-turn in perspective (the literal meaning of *peripeteia!*) Fred is finally able to relax and becomes emotional in a different way: calm, moved, grateful and slightly embarrassed about a case that is not his own.

I make up my mind and agree with Fred that I will e-mail him again in four months or so to find out how the *denouement* (phase 4!) part of his case went. I am full of confidence and convinced that the situation will no longer present a problem by then. Imagine my surprise when it turns out that very little has changed (I quote literally from Fred's e-mail, only changing the names): "And then the *people management case*, I haven't really made any progress there. Let's be clear: Lex certainly didn't go up in the popularity ratings in that discussion. And all Piet did in the discussion was mention the results achieved by Lex in the past, so that didn't really make the situation any better either. Briefly, how did I get on . . . now I am simply older and a bit wiser in terms of experience and as to the case itself I mainly leave it as it is."

At least two aspects are recognisable to the tragic consultant: (1) the *case*, the problem, is still exactly as it was, despite all of the consulting work by colleagues from the auction house and the external consultant, and (2) the client is now sadder and wiser and (at times) reconciles himself with the case. Could the consultant have done things differently and better? I am sure. Would the outcome have been very different? That remains the question.

Three months from now, I will have my last involvement with the consultation group (phase 5!), a sort of reflection after a full year of the group facilitating itself. I am very curious to see how it will go – a *catastrophe* or an enthusiastic goodbye?!

What pleasure does a tragedy give?

Let us now return to Nietzsche's answer to the question posed at the outset. In the first place, Nietzsche had to relate anew to Aristotle (*Poetica*, 4th century BC), who had given a very influential, albeit short, answer. Aristotle says that tragedy strips suffering, which is its subject, of its repugnant nature by arousing compassion and fear in the spectator (49b27[11]).

Nietzsche (1872) breaks completely with this view by claiming that tragedy brings us not the pleasure of the phenomena but the pleasure *behind* the phenomena. He maintains that it is only *despite* compassion and fear that we are able to enjoy the insight that everything that has been created must be prepared to suffer in a tragic way.[12] If we can discern behind the jumble of phenomena, actions and situations how life carries on regardless, it comes as a comfort to us. According to Nietzsche, it is that comfort that provides us with enormous pleasure.

Here again, Nietzsche's ideas translate very well to consulting. "Everything which rises to the surface in the Apollonian part of Greek tragedy, in the dialogue, looks simple, transparent, and beautiful . . ." (Nietzsche, 1872) can be translated to "Everything our clients say to each other, to themselves and to us sounds neat, ordered, reasonable . . ." and Nietzsche continues: "But once we turn our gaze in a powerful attempt to stare at this sun, we turn away blinded with dark spots before our eyes." The "dark spots" in the stories and behaviours of our clients betray tragic undercurrents and a deep suffering that they themselves, certainly in the workplace, are unwilling to examine.

---

11 Bookshelves full of books have been written about this short passage in Aristotle. It has raised many more questions than it has answered. For example, it is not clear whether Aristotle, by *catharsis*, means ridding ourselves of or purifying strong emotions. What *is* clear is that Aristotle writes that tragedy works *by* arousing compassion and fear and not *despite* compassion and fear, as Nietzsche has it. Whatever interpretation we choose, Nietzsche is in strong opposition to Aristotle.

12 So, clearly, Nietzsche does share Aristotle's view that watching a painful reality leads to *insight* and that this learning brings us pleasure (compare also *Poetica*, 48b10).

It is therefore often a consolation for the consultant to continue to watch, not to allow himself to be overcome by compassion or fear, and to study how the dark spots form unmistakable patterns, merge together, separate again, keep resurfacing and distort and knock down the clear, reasonable, unambiguous stories.

When we feel this consolation, which goes beyond the events, and start to work with the imperturbability of the undercurrent of our clients' stories, there are always three obvious possible options according to Nietzsche (1872, preface from 1886):
1. *Resignation*, where the situation is taken as further evidence to the tragic state of our condition;
2. *Metaphysical consolation* in the form of worship and romanticism;
3. *The consolation of this world*, by positively choosing the outcomes of the tragic fate.

In his later works Nietzsche pleads strongly in favour of the last option, which he sums up in the Latin phrase *amor fati*: "Love your fate." Another way of summarising it can be found in *Thus Spake Zarathustra* (1885), in his fervent desire to be an ass, the animal that says "yes" under all circumstances.

Responsibility (see Chapter 8) now takes on a different meaning and begins to soar above human limitations and powers: responsibility here expresses itself in forgiveness and compassion, also with respect to one's own tragedy. Moreover, as a consultant one always recognises something of one's own tragedy in the tragedy of others, and that makes it easier to have compassion.

Conclusion

An awareness or lack of awareness of tragic undercurrents in an Apollonian reality has significant consequences, in my experience, for one's contribution as a consultant and the intention that is so essential in consulting. As a result, I think it useful to go through all of the possibilities one by one:
1. *No awareness of tragic undercurrents*. All too often, the consultant and client together have no awareness of or feeling for the tragic aspects of a problem. The *intention* is often naively optimistic, unassuming and hopeful: "If we just do our best, it will all work out

well", or: "Sure, this has gone wrong frequently in the past, but we're now going to tackle it with an entirely new method."

2. *Not making use of tragic undercurrents.* Lawrence (2000) describes in his final chapter on *Tragedy* how professionals tend to recoil when they discern tragic patterns and try to pretend those patterns do not exist. "Tragedy (ranging from disappointment through loss to death) is construed by people as an intrusion in their lives, an impertinence of fate. Tragedy, we have come to believe, is not supposed to happen and is to be wished away. Life should be trouble-free. Because we believe that man is superior to everything else that exists on earth and is, therefore, god-like, we have no means of integrating tragedy into our lives. Tragedy we 'split off' onto characters in films and television drama, and into the weak and the 'under-classes'." (Lawrence, 2000). Clients and consultants can sustain this for a long time, but in the end their consulting process and functioning will suffer.

   Of course, there are also cases where we do not *need* to make use of tragic undercurrents and can leave them as they are, simply because we do not have to intervene at that depth. In a one-off expert consultation or a short coaching programme, for example, it is perhaps unnecessary and even counterproductive to address the tragic aspects. Very often, however, the client wants to make us believe that there are no existential doubts or tragedies at issue, or we ourselves hope that it is not all too difficult, while such tragic undercurrents do indeed come into play.

3. *Abusing tragic undercurrents.* Unfortunately, it often happens that consultants suspect tragic undercurrents and conveniently take advantage of them. We see this primarily in advertising statements by consultants and in the way in which they present themselves in entry conversations. For some particularly stark examples, such as "selling by creating client dependency", "promising upfront to save 30% of costs or to implement new strategies, whatever they are" or "blowing your project's scope", see the book *Rip-off!* (Craig, 2005). These consultants present their clients with magic promises and doom scenarios, with the auxiliary aim of making those clients dependent on their expertise. More examples can be found in Pinault (2000). In Holland, I have noticed this perverted intention in recent years in relation to the theme of acquisition itself: an increase in training courses, lectures and books, while the underlying tragedy – a market in miserable decline – is not "dealt with" or even made explicit.

When tragic undercurrents are abused, the intention of consulting becomes manipulative and sly, and the consultant easily loses sight of the client's interests.

4. *Resignation in the face of tragic undercurrents.* This intention is strongly advocated by Schopenhauer (1819): "What gives tragedy its curious uplifting momentum, is the dawning of the knowledge that the world, that life can offer no real satisfaction and as a result does not merit our devotion: this is the essence of the tragic spirit – it leads accordingly to resignation." The development of the consulting *state of mind*, which says that we try to be attentive to the here and now, and to note what is happening (see the prologue to this book), certainly contributes to such a resigned intention. Obviously, it is possible that this stoical intention may lead to cynicism, scepticism or nihilism. However, this need not mean that the intention of the consulting process becomes perverted. As long as the consultant continues to speak fearlessly about it, to listen attentively to the client's response and is able to let go of his own doubts without letting go of the client, it is still possible, even in the face of cynicism, scepticism and nihilism, to intervene in a healing and helping manner.

5. *Optimism in the face of tragic undercurrents.* This is the romantic answer to the tragic experience, often expressed as an enlightened optimism: "I'm not able to handle it well yet, but possibly later." Nietzsche refers in this connection to the *Sehnsucht zum Idyll* (yearning for the idyllic), which characterises so much modern drama and opera. The consultant's intention is now optimistic, but cautious. This intention may give way to escapism: helping the client to "forget" his own tragic experiences. Hypnotic approaches to consulting, which may stem from a Dionysian rapture, often contribute in this respect.

6. Amor fati *in the face of tragic undercurrents.* This is, as we have said, the approach consistently recommended by Nietzsche in all of his books: it is the actual seeking out of anxiety and doubt itself, precisely in order to learn what they are. This results in a pessimistic, but exploratory intention. Freud (1912b) asks the consultant to model himself on the surgeon, who puts aside his emotions and sympathy and makes it his sole aim to carry out the operation as skilfully as possible.[13] This certainly does not mean – according to Nietzsche as well – that you as a consultant are gloomy, dramatic

---

13 Under the surgeon's motto *Je le pansai, Dieu le guerrit* (Freud, 1912b).

or heavy-handed: *amor fati* is in fact very light, playful and transparent in practice. The aim is to be aware of decisive undercurrents in the client's attitude and behaviour and to be prepared to discuss them with the client.

I am firmly convinced that the client in most consulting processes, even in short consulting conversations, is best served by a consultant who is at least aware of the tragic and has some knowledge of his own attitude towards the tragic. The *tragic consultant* is alert to the tragic undercurrents in the client and in himself, and practises letting go as a tool to enable him to continue consulting. The tragic consultant also has some idea of his own intention as the result of the tragic: how sensitive is he to abuse of the tragic? And on the other hand: how tempting is it for him to wallow in the tragic?

We can imagine tragic consulting at the mid-point of a sliding scale with "resignation" and "rapture" at either end. The consultant attempts to achieve mastery by staying away from these extremes and feeling comfortable in the middle zone, finding a tragic attitude in a variety of situations.

♪

Summary: letting go and tragic consulting

Letting go of the consulting process and the consulting relationship takes some effort. Often, the quality of letting go is related to the ability of the consultant to **let go of oneself**: to put aside one's own needs and not to take oneself too seriously.

Ideally, the consultant practises the art of letting go throughout the consulting assignment – letting go, that is, without reducing his own sensitivity, empathy and involvement.

We recognise the consultant who lets go in the **chorus in Greek tragedy**. Members of the chorus appear in many consulting roles, which share in common at least the following activities:
- Making explicit, reflecting and re-framing (metaphor of the garment);
- Surrounding, containing and providing for (metaphor of the living wall);
- Witnessing, lamenting and reconciling (metaphor of countenancing the upset of emotions).

In the face of tragedy a consultant has the following options:
- Not to be aware of it;
- Not to make use of it, and to ignore it;
- To abuse it;
- To resign to it;
- To be optimistic about it;
- To seek it for further understanding (**amor fati**).

The **tragic consultant**
- is aware of the inevitable in the client;
- is aware of the inevitable in himself, such as enchantment, needs and impulses;
- asks himself why he actually became a consultant, so is aware of his own **helper's syndrome**;
- continues to consult fearlessly even without hope of success;
- embraces his own fate and is able to opt actively for doubt, dejection and despair;
- draws satisfaction from the "eternal recurrence of the unavoidable".

Enjoying tragic consulting is therefore entirely possible. If you can learn to say "yes", even to the greatest failure, disillusionment and doubt, you are already half-way there.

Epilogue: Twenty Minutes in the Life of a Consultant

The invitation

"Hendrik, I've got something to ask you, something I'd like to do with you. But take your time to decide if it appeals to you too.

I want to write a sort of epilogue for my book, in which I bring a number of strands together and test some assumptions about consulting. Not in the form of an ordinary chapter, more in the form of a "detailed observation" of a real consulting conversation. So I'm looking for someone who is prepared to hold a real consulting conversation with me, which will be recorded. The intention is that we both make notes about what is happening within ourselves and what we think is happening within the other person, as openly, honestly and fully as possible. The notes start even before the conversation, then continue during the conversation, and flow on after the conversation. We exchange these notes and each make new notes about what the original notes trigger in ourselves – and possibly in the other person as well. We then get together again to discuss all of the notes, and I edit the texts into a not-too-long cohesive chapter.

Hendrik, it's great that you're going to do it! It's an advantage that you're not familiar with the content of the book. Now for a few ideas about the conversation itself:
- I'm looking for a consulting conversation about a "real" (i.e. relevant, timely, urgent) and work-related subject, so it can be about your projects or perhaps your own role at work, it can be specific or broad, sharply defined or vague, as long as it's "real"!
- I think it would be a good idea if we both write out two A4 sheets with our thoughts, expectations, doubts, hopes, etc., prior to the conversation.

- The conversation need only take half an hour or so, I'll probably type out only 15 minutes' worth, word for word.
- I would prefer to do a sort of "double left-hand column", if you know what I mean: I would like as many notes as possible about (1) what is going on in yourself during the conversation and (2) what you think is going on inside me during the conversation. If necessary we can both scribble something down immediately after the conversation.
- I also think it's a good idea to note down a few things afterwards, about the impact of the conversation (if any . . .).
- For the moment, therefore, I am looking for three narratives: before, during and after the conversation – three narratives centring on yourself in relation to me. You can deliver them to me in short bullet points in the week (or weeks) after the conversation, then I'll copy them out. You can certainly also "interpret" in the sense of "I think this therefore probably X is going on within me", or "he says this, therefore he is probably thinking about Y".
- It will probably help if I work out the literal text soon after the conversation, because more ideas may occur to you while you are reading it.
- When we both have our ideas ready, we will e-mail them to each other and then hold a rounding-off conversation with reflections-on-reflections.

You'd prefer to contribute a confidential issue, and then make it anonymous for the book? I quite understand. I suggest that I rework the subject of the conversation in order to make it confidential, and if you're not happy with it we can make further adjustments."

Observations prior to the conversation

1. The client's observations: based on Hendrik's notes
This is a nice opportunity to do something together with Erik. I haven't talked with him for a while. I don't expect it will change my current ideas fundamentally.

I have chosen a real problem, but I will actually have to deal with it before the conversation. It is my most tangible issue at the moment, but it may be cleared up by next week, although I don't really expect it to be.

It concerns my project in which I am collaborating with Bernadette, and I don't think she's suitable as project coordinator. Maybe Erik will think my current idea of recommending that Bernadette be taken off the project is overly severe and unreasonable.

But yes, taking someone off a project, so taking responsibility for someone else's performance, is a recurring theme for me, with a heavy emotional burden due to what once happened to my sister. I kept coming up against it in my previous position, and now again. When is it fair to remove someone from his post or take him off a project?

This kind of thing affected me deeply, for example, in a project for my previous employer when I took the initiative to tell Ria that we weren't happy with her contribution.

What I really wonder is: is this really just taking responsibility for my role as a fellow professional? Or is it actually more about me than about her? I think that's always an important criterion: if it's more about me it's a bit suspicious. And now I wonder above all: will Erik agree or will he see things very differently? And: are we going to repeat my whole psychological journey again? I know that bit of myself. Do I really have to keep going through it again and again, or will something change, perhaps the colouring of the emotion?

So I feel unsure about my decision, but we will probably both be unsure. We know about each other's professionalism but haven't yet experienced anything of it. I suspect I will do my best to prove to Erik that everything I do has been considered thoroughly.

Anyway, what can 15 minutes of consulting conversation actually change? Perhaps my train of thought at that moment, but that doesn't mean my actions will be radically different. And, incidentally, that's not really necessary because I am reasonably satisfied with the way I handle these situations, in general. I am fairly intense and direct in my collaboration with others. Desirée found out as much in February. She bolted like a startled animal after our first real confrontation.

How will the consulting conversation go? Have I got the courage to show the real me, or will I put on a show because I also know Erik in a different capacity?

2. The consultant's observations: based on Erik's notes
What is Hendrik going to come up with? Will I be able to understand
where he's coming from? Will I be able to help him with his problem?
We're both consultants, so there's a good chance that he'll come up
with something that I recognise. Will that recognition facilitate the
consulting process or get in the way? For me there is always an associated doubt about whether I will be "good enough" as a consultant . . .

Have I already noticed something about his problem before the first
conversation? Yes: the phone call about confidentiality. He was keen
to bring up a real issue, but was concerned about how I would handle
the confidentiality aspect. He doesn't want his "issue" to appear in the
book as is. This means, in any case, that we are going to be talking
about something that really concerns him, but it also means that he is
slightly apprehensive about what I'm going to do with it, and whether
I'm going to run off with his problem.

How will I come across? I don't think I've ever really advised Hendrik
before; we don't have that sort of relationship. Now it has been
"decided" in advance that we are going to have a consulting conversation, and that means he has to put himself in the role of client. Will
he accept me as consultant during the conversation? Will he try to put
me to the test? Or, on the contrary, will he try to help me too much,
perhaps by responding favourably to interventions that don't actually
appeal to him? Will he be kind to me because the aim of the entire
conversation is to help me and my book? I wonder if I'll manage to
speak fearlessly to Hendrik right from the start: our relationship is very
open and relaxed, but also friendly and respectful. Perhaps there will
be moments when I feel I should say something that sounds a bit less
friendly. Perhaps he'll seduce me into coming up with all sorts of solutions and suggestions. After all, that is the only form of consulting that
has existed between us to date, a form of expert consulting. Whereas
a different role might be more appropriate here.

And then: what sort of consulting conversation is this in fact? It is
stage-managed, it is not based on an initiative on his part, so how can
it ever be a good example for the readers of this book? Perhaps we'll
both just be pretending, or on the other hand perhaps we'll just be
doing our very best to make it a fascinating conversation for the book
and its readers.

What can I expect? Something about a project, probably, or about his own career as a consultant. Two days before our conversation he sends me his "preliminary observations" with a request not to read them ("Don't read them on the sly, eh?", he writes). Right away, that is his first ironic, even paradoxical message, as in: "Don't read what is written here." He is in any case an intriguing client, because I do indeed have to restrain myself from looking at the document I have received.

Irony often points to ambivalences in the issue. Maybe the message here is: look at me, advise me, and at the same time: don't see too much of me, and don't let this become a one-sided consulting relationship (he's already giving me advice in advance!). This sort of ambivalence is often a sign of commitment, as is the early sending in of his preliminary ideas. You can rely on Hendrik for doing his homework, that much is clear.

My final thought on the basis of his e-mail is that this "client" evidently sees the consulting process much less as a process than I do: he thinks he can round off his preliminary ideas two days before the conversation actually takes place. In my case I continue to make notes throughout the run-up to the consulting conversation, always adding new ideas, including thoughts that appear to deny or contradict my earlier thoughts.

The evening before our appointment, the telephone rings. My first thought is: Hendrik! And indeed, I am right. He wants to confirm the time. And he's not feeling well, is going to bed early. I don't know how I am supposed to connect this to our conversation. I do notice that I don't say: "If you're not feeling well, we'll just do it another time." I am evidently much too keen to do it tomorrow, I'm much too curious. Later I send him a text message to put this right and then wait with bated breath to find out if the conversation is going ahead. This is something that happens a lot with other new clients as well: endless liaising and manoeuvring before we actually meet.

What do I notice in myself? Actually, the same tension I usually feel before a conversation with a new client. A sort of emotional alertness and readiness, as if I'm about to embark on an adventure full of uncertainties. I am keen to be there for him and his problems. I hope that I can drop this fretting and stewing before we start, that I can forget that all of this has been organised for a book. That I can be "without memory and desire", as Bion once wrote.

Self-reflection and self-monitoring: consultant and client subject their consulting conversation to a detailed examination. They pin down every word and every gesture and try to discover their meanings and effects together.

The conversation as it took place

The conversation that took place in December 2004 is reproduced as completely and faithfully as possible, including interjections and extended silences. In the following, there are some highlights from the first 17 minutes of the conversation, containing the only words uttered by the consultant, and then from "intervention number 1" the verbatim text is unaltered and uninterrupted until "intervention number 79", comprising exactly 20 minutes. Abbreviations used:

Co:	consultant (Erik)
Cl:	client (Hendrik)
*:	extended silence
–:	after a word, means interrupted, sometimes by the speaker himself and sometimes by the other person
(. . .):	text omitted, sometimes up to several minutes' worth
0′:	passage of time during the conversation, in minutes

0′	Co	. . . I will make some notes if that's ok with you.
	Cl	Shall I do that as well? (. . .)
	Co	OK. What would you like to talk about?
1′	Cl	Well, what I'd like to contribute is a situation relating to a project that I've just acquired together with (. . .)
11′	Co	An "experience of loss"? What – ?
	Cl	Well, Bernadette clearly feels that more and more of her work is being taken away from her and that she's increasingly being overruled by her boss (. . .)
		But you can't do it alone, you can't write an action plan by yourself.
14′	Co	So you are saying that you thought to yourself, I have to take charge, but you said to her, we have to take charge together. Because –
	Cl	Um, well, in our heads we were thinking or in my head I was thinking how are you going to handle that with Bernadette in the broadest sense of the word
	Co	Yes
15′	Cl	The minimum, the bottom line in this is (. . .)
		The reason I bring this up is because I think, and this has often been an issue for me and then it is purely about taking responsibility for, what do I take responsibility for? And uh do I do that on account of a project or does it mainly have to do with myself?
		That's a very long introduction I think –
1	Co	Yes, it is certainly quite a story and –
17′	Cl	And that problem is very real, though in this case there is a solution –
2	Co	There seems to be – yes, yes, I understand, you want to focus mainly on the latter in this conversation, on, as you say, what am I responsible for taking on here?
	Cl	Yes, and uh let's say professionally, in the professional environment.
3	Co	Can you also say something about, um, what your goal is, in raising that issue? In German they have a very good word for it, Anliegen: what is at stake for you here?
	Cl	* um, well, what is at stake are relationships with people, so how I develop professional relationships?
4	Co	Yes
	Cl	Mm, and so also relationships in the broadest sense of the word, um or no, not the relationships but professionalism in the broadest sense of the word, your relationships with people are an important element of your professionalism. It's a recurring theme for me, I notice that it always affects me deeply when it comes up, so a very simple, different example is, I had in my team at the Company a professional who simply wasn't good enough and that that that I do plainly address with a person, or one, I had two of them, one a consultant and that affected me most because they were very intense conversations
5	Co	Hm hm
	Cl	and one person in support. And um well what is one's – and I think that this that that Anliegen has to do with, um, how you're seen by other people because you take responsibility

6   Co   And who –

      Cl   for something but also for someone at that moment, because it is just about a person, you don't take your responsibility for something but my something is that programme that I have to organise. The Business says organise a programme not dismiss a person. That's not my responsibility.

7   Co   Yes so it isn't and who – when you say how other people see me, what other people are you referring to in this instance?

      Cl   Well

8   Co   Do you mean Bernadette mainly, or do you mean Barbara mainly, or –

      Cl   No, I am thinking mainly about, um, Bernadette, there's also someone else in the picture, someone called Nicole who supports her

9   Co   Yes, yes, course

      Cl   and Siert, who manages her, and what all of those people think

10 Co   Yes

      Cl   and that is all quite independent of the good intentions that one may have in what one says or intends,

11 Co   Yes, yes

      Cl   what I say or intend therefore when I say –

12 Co   Independent of your own good intentions

      Cl   Yes

13 Co   might they think very badly of you?

      Cl   Yes

14 Co   that's a yes?

      Cl   Yes

15 Co   and that affects you, if that were the case would it affect you? You say it affects me.

      Cl   Yes, that affects me mainly, I think, if I am misunderstood as a result, if there's another um, um –

16 Co   Yes, and how would you want to use this conversation or myself, in that Anliegen in what you have just said very clearly in my opinion?

      Cl   * um, well, I think by mirroring and by helping to reflect on that, placing it in a wider context etc.

17 Co   um * uh What do you mean by a wider context? Do you mean as I mean, because we know each other of course from before this conversation, do you mean any relationships with how I perceive you, or do you mean a wider context? –

21′ Cl   Yes, possibly

18 Co   Possibly?

      Cl   Possibly, I don't find it complicated I don't know if it's difficult for you because um because well that is – fine no that is fine um yes as such

19 Co   Yes, as such um * well what would be interesting would perhaps be to continue reflecting on a few things that you have said and I would also be able to give something back, perhaps I'll have to wait a bit um you say a recurring theme and you say that it has something to do with responsibility.

      Cl   Hm hm

20 Co   And I find that, I find that interesting um and you also say something about uh how other people see you,

      Cl   Hm hm

21   Co   so I notice that you connect those things.

       Cl   Yes, yes

22   Co   Perhaps the most interesting thing for me is to start with that recurring theme,

       Cl   Yes

23   Co   um well if that doesn't – if you want you could by all means say something more about it, but could you say something about where it recurs specifically? um

       Cl   Yes

24   Co   You have already given one example of when you yourself were managing others –

       Cl   When I was managing, well, within the Company it was even more visible in fact in the ambiguity of all roles, so there wasn't much visible there, or no, there wasn't much appointed leadership or people in clear roles so even before I became sector manager um I took I also accepted that responsibility for both projects and people, I tell people when things are going well but I also tell people when things are not going well in my experience, and I also realise well enough that my experience is only one experience, so I relied strongly on principles of client management: if a client thinks it's OK I am not going to go looking for conflict. um

25   Co   Hm hm

       Cl   But I am always someone that you will meet in this and, or that you will – yes that that is um very clear in this and um in those days when we were for example sitting together with a team of four project leaders, all four of whom were leading the Project and when I then, if everyone in a team thinks that one of them isn't performing well, not getting on well, I think it's our responsibility as a team that that person should know it um

26   Co   Yes

25′   Cl   and in my experience for two reasons, you know, um the first reason um if we as a team think something we should just say it, because otherwise no-one can learn from it, they can't take responsibility for something they're not aware of and the other side is for the person that happens to, that other people think he's not up to the job for whatever reason, is entitled to know how people view him moreover one can be very stuck in a thought of something going well when actually it isn't working so it can be very liberating, in the end, to

27   Co   Yes

       Cl   to be aware of why something isn't working etc.

28   Co   Yes

       Cl   well, that is the recurring theme and that is also the time when it became most visible, that's interesting that's about the relationship with um with Barbara. This came up very clearly in connection with a Project Day, so we had a Project Team, managers responsible for the Project, there was indeed one of them who wasn't performing well um, who was also fairly blind to all of the signals there were, because there were signals, clearly didn't pick them up, was a pretty thick-skinned, abrasive woman. We had our professional development day and uh via all of the subtle signals it was made clear to her not to come.

29 Co Hm

Cl As can sometimes happen in a consultant's environment, so it was, everything was ambiguous but it was clear that Ria didn't belong there and uh, I don't like that, I think if there's something wrong, be clear about it and Ria 'course, Ria came anyway, because if you don't have a clear understanding, there were four or five of us there, four people were very bothered by it, I wasn't as bothered as the others, but I was bothered by it you know, so I was bothered by it but I am bothered by it but I see Ria is bothered too so I and I look at this going on, so I think well, if it's an issue just bring it up, and then we, what I remember is we had had a "preliminary moment", a preliminary conversation over drinks, no over dinner, Ria went home, to see to the children, when I said to everyone what are we going to do here, this should be brought up, at some time, no, that was at snack time because she was eating with us, then we said it in the evening, everyone thought we should talk about it, and I said "Well, I'll say something, but you support me or back me up so that it's not just me speaking,"

30 Co Hm

Cl "but you say what you think, because I mean if it's only me speaking we shouldn't do it."

31 Co Yes

Cl And then we all sat there and then I remember well it was a lovely summer evening, just like this is such a quiet period at the end of the year

32 Co Yes yes

Cl similarly in the summertime in the Company: on the terrace the five of us outside with a drink and we entered into that conversation with Ria, I said a few things very clearly I think, so intensely and insistently and the rest of the group were virtually silent. And that may have had to do with the fact that I am speaking so intensely and insistently, that they think oh my god there's nothing more I can add to that.

33 Co Yes, I see, yes

Cl And that had a sequel, the first sequel was that I drove home in the evening and then thought oh my god what have I done and the next morning, no during the night I dreamed that the sheets were hanging out of the window of the room where she slept and that she had either committed suicide or uh, I don't know what, something like that and the next morning it was fairly intense as well because she had indeed gone and she was uh and she was really angry with the team uh and I don't know what, "ridiculous" and so on. Although I can handle that rationally reasonably well

34 Co Hm

Cl I notice that it affects me in a way that –

35 Co Yes. And that you're full of all sorts of doubts.

Cl Yes, then I think, who am I doing this for?

36 Co Yes and am I doing this – In my view, everything you are saying is very strongly connected with, um with, in any case it strikes me as a strongly ethical issue, you use words such as principles, responsibility, helping someone, being able to liberate someone, all of these seem to me to be very ethical terms.

28′ Cl Hm
37 Co And I get the idea, from all of the examples you give, that yours is a great struggle with integrity and the proper handling of ethical issues.
    Cl Yes
38 Co And –
    Cl But in my experience this is also the essence of management professions, when you're dealing with performance management then –
39 Co Yes if you indeed refer to ethics as as as a field of study, but I also recognise the personal element, the personal aspect of that struggle.
    Cl Yes
40 Co Perhaps it's a good idea to focus on that for a while, of course this is also something that is described in books,
    Cl Yes
41 Co but now you experience it as an ethical dilemma or as a, more as a second thought, along the lines of "I have done something, I have exerted a great influence, um, but what will people think of me . . . "
    Cl Hm hm (agreeing)
42 Co . . . and did I actually behave properly, however much I wanted to? And what I am hearing strongly is, I hear recurring things and I, I do indeed find reasons in your account to think badly of you if I want to, and I think that is also the doubt that you have, because if those thoughts occur to me then they also occur to you.
    Cl Hm hm
43 Co Um so you stick your neck out uh in all of your accounts and there is also something about, I think, maybe being unfair, or taking unfair advantage. Um I don't know if you recognise it but um what you, what you refer to starts right away with the acquisition of that assignment, where you when you look at it in accordance with the ethical codes of conduct I think um, when you voice an opinion about another consultant there are a number of articles about that and what you did is not ultimately permitted within most ethical codes, now you haven't adhered to specific ethical codes, but I think you do experience similar matters
    Cl Hm hm yes
44 Co that someone perhaps could be very – and you have said as much
    Cl Yes
45 Co Later, um in the case of that woman, Bernadette, um perhaps I brought it up a bit prematurely, that you, that you yourself were thinking about taking charge, a need to take charge in order to be able to do something,
    Cl Hm hm
46 Co and said to her: taking charge together, there's a sort of discrepancy there
30′ Cl Hm hm
47 Co "Am I entirely transparent and open? I stand for them, for those principles, of clearness and clarity, but am I succeeding in that?" And the other thing is, taking unfair advantage, in a certain sense, just like the winning of the project, is that you actually discussed a lot more with Siert than with Bernadette, and there too, in my view, there are also principles, that you um can say something about someone in assignments only if it's part of the

assignment and if you have first said it to that person, now that too is, can be for me and for all other onlookers a reason for thinking badly of you, and so I suspect that you also have that in yourself:

Cl   Hm hm

48 Co a part of you, a voice that says "am I acting with integrity?", and another voice that also comes through very strongly saying "Yes, I am the person taking responsibility here, I am the person doing the dirty work, taking um the irons out of the fire, um taking the chestnuts out of the fire for other people." The last example, but also in the last example I think that you yourself have doubts whether this conversation with Ria, whether it should have been a conversation in a group around a table over drinks, or rather a conversation between two people, between the Project owner and um Ria herself,

Cl   Hm hm

49 Co as two individuals, so I'm hearing a lot of doubts, um struggles and also um the possibility of thinking very badly of yourself. Do I understand that right, or . . .?

Cl   Um * Well, that is not so much as far as I am concerned, not so much an understanding but it is more your interpretation,

50 Co Hm hm

Cl   so you, in my experience you are making it look blacker than I see it myself,

51 Co Yes

Cl   but that can also be resistance. I don't know that sort of rules very well, the formal rules surrounding ethics and um and um for example talking about someone

52 Co Hm hm

Cl   From the context of an assignment or the extent to which that can be taken more broadly. Certainly with Bernadette in the run-up, in what we had gone through together in the space of four weeks, there was more than enough substance to raise that, and also discuss with her, not everything, not everything by one person at the right moment, before it was discussed with Siert, but virtually everything has been up for discussion with her,

53 Co Hm

Cl   um but broadly speaking yes there has been yes that –

54 Co So I'm rambling, I'm giving you what you asked for, uh that, reflecting that, but I distort in my reflection, would you say?

Cl   * Well, it's interesting in any case to observe how you just, how you person-ally think about it, because it makes you respond intensely too

55 Co Hm hm hm

Cl   And yes it's about an ethical issue and it's about integrity. And my integrity is never – So I find it very interesting that you refer for example to rules about this, I'm not very familiar with those rules in any case, and um

56 Co But you do have the same doubts? The same doubts as –

34′ Cl Yes yes yes that's interesting so I am much more along the um I was, I was inclined to say that I am never so quick to take rules as my starting point, I am not the sort of person who waits around at a red traffic light in the middle of the night,

57 Co Hm hm
    Cl but I do think it important not to hurt anyone with my driving behaviour.
58 Co Yes
    Cl And I am someone who does take some advantage, indeed. Then there are reasons for other people to think badly of me, yes, if you look at it that way then this is just very matter-of-fact, a metaphor, which is is is most true, I must get used to the way in which you refer to it and how you –
59 Co What is happening here is also that um, in one way or another this conversation in my view is starting to resemble, um certainly the way in which you now understand it, as if I am now the person who does the same as you do in those examples, namely saying very clearly listen up Hendrik, you're not performing.
    Cl Hm hm
60 Co That's almost what it's starting to resemble in this conversation.
    Cl Yes
61 Co So it's as if I am taking over your role and as a matter of fact I am now suddenly getting all sorts of doubts: I don't recognise that you say I respond intensely, I am um intrigued about the sort of questions and I also recognise your doubts, because I immediately have the doubt: um "Oops, should I have said it like that?"
    Cl Hm hm
62 Co "What is Hendrik going to think about me now?"
    Cl Yes
63 Co "After me speaking out like this?"
    Cl Yes
64 Co "Because he now thinks of course that I think that he is taking unfair advantage and stepping all over the rules
    Cl Yes
65 Co and trampling on them, and so on." So I am ending up in the same position in a way
    Cl Yes
66 Co like you in that –
    Cl Yes and it doesn't have to come to a stalemate because it takes, costs me a bit of time and then I can, then it is great to hear this sort of thing, rather than when someone tries with a gentle touch and velvety glove to answer
67 Co Yes
    Cl with a subtle reflection,
68 Co Yes
    Cl so I learn here, I learn more because I really get your – also
69 Co Yes
    Cl partly your opinion back, and think "O sh . . . , so simple and still so intense is also your response" – because I do find your response to this really intense –
70 Co Yes yes
    Cl And um and this ultimately does work for me and I need some thinking time but uh for example –

71	Co	But I think –
	Cl	An example, one of the answers is
72	Co	Yes
	Cl	what works for me is not always necessarily what works for someone else, so we tend, in feedback we tend, in feedback I often tend to think that the way I do this will also be good for others,
73	Co	Yes
	Cl	while that's not what it's about at all
74	Co	Yes, and what is happening now is not great at all for you and as a result it is also not great for – What I actually do I think –
	Cl	Yes, but that's not the issue because that is one
75	Co	Yes
37′	Cl	of the great confusions surrounding this sort of – it's never great to hear this sort of thing, Erik.
76	Co	No
	Cl	Of course, it's not great for Bernadette to hear that "We'll deliver a better project if you're not there than if you are there", that's a bloody awful message, that I understand very well.
77	Co	Yes
	Cl	You know that is also –
78	Co	With repercussions for yourself, so I – What? Sorry – * You wanted to say something else?
	Cl	Yes, because it touches on, because it touches on the theme, perhaps I'm not doing this right, um it's about discovering one's own limits, so it's about taking responsibility for someone and discovering one's limits, in this case for Bernadette discovering the limits of "Gee, is an international business an environment where I can work well and make a contribution?", and it is easy enough for me to say "Gee, it is important that we all take responsibility for our lives and that we do our best to add value to the place where we belong and that we are a bit lucky and happy to be there, and my manager has an important . . ." – You know, that's all philosophical but at the most essential level I come across the fact that my – and there, there it touches of course on the personal relationships, that my sister has much fewer opportunities than I do and (. . .) Can you imagine that?
79	Co	Yes, I can imagine that because I've been thinking about your sister for a few minutes so I'm glad you mention her now.
40′		(. . .)
50′		*End of the conversation*

The conversation as it did not take place

The following is an impression of the conversation that did not take place, at least not explicitly, but only implicitly: in the minds of client and consultant. The following text is based on the notes made by consultant and client immediately after the end of the conversation, in which they expressed their ideas and feelings during the conversation as candidly as possible. The intervention numbers are the same as in the explicit conversation above. The dialogue below therefore gives an insight into the underlying, unspoken "subtext" in the minds of client and consultant.

Start	Cl	I find the comment "Now, when I return I enter as your consultant" peculiar: what does that mean? Are you going to behave differently from normal? For me it's very important to "be able to be myself" when I am a consultant.
	Cl	The artificial feeling at the start soon disappears, fortunately, during the conversation. I now feel I have space to tell my story.
	Co	What an introduction! What power! What details! I've been sitting here for a while thinking about ethics and integrity – how am I going to bring that up?
	Cl	I've been talking for a good 15 minutes, creating context and telling the story. He's watching with a sombre and serious expression. That makes me insecure. Is what I'm telling him really so bad? It helps (even if only symbolically) that he's writing things down, it makes me feel I'm being listened to and taken seriously.
2	Co	I'm pleased that this is about responsibility! I observe an unusual combination of pride and insecurity in him.
	Cl	I notice he's writing down the word leadership. That's certainly what it's about at the moment.
3	Co	What does he mean, is he delimiting the conversation? Is this distinction between "personal" and "professional" significant for him? Is he afraid it will become too personal for him? I want to get to the "gut feeling", to what is at stake for him. I notice that I am set to concentrate on what is most personal.
	Cl	His question about *Anliegen* and how he can be of help with that, helps me to structure what I can get out of this.
4	Co	It's all so general. He talks about "professionalism" – but surely that's not specific enough for a consulting conversation?
5	Co	Aha, a recurring theme. That means that we're getting "open doors" through to patterns of issues that are relevant for Hendrik, and that we can therefore automatically be on the lookout for the underpinning issues in these patterns.
6	Co	He wonders how people perceive him: this brings us already to an underlying issue – in fact, a universal human theme – good, we can focus on that.
8	Co	Let's see if we can get even more specific.
15	Co	Even more specific. And let's not avoid the emotions.
16	Co	What does he expect? What is he looking for?
	Cl	Precisely this question about his role as a consultant gives me influence over the structure of the conversation and makes my expectations clear as well.

17	Co	Hey, I'm making it more personal here than he perhaps intended. This seems to be causing a sort of tension in him, some feeling of embarrassment, perhaps.
22	Co	Am I too directive?
25	Co	He enjoys talking about this. And I find him very articulate; in this way he comes across again as being proud of his approach, and of his well-considered motivation.
26	Co	Now it seems to be turning into a bit of a flat conversation.
30	Co	Sounds harsh the way he talks about that woman. And yes, unfortunately, that is the way it is in some consultants' environments . . . He's still speaking with pride, and with enthusiasm, and also with a sort of irritation towards others in that situation.
32	Co	I notice that I respond enthusiastically to the connection that he makes to the here and now, to this conversation here between us. As if he involves me more in it again.
34	Co	Look at this: a dream. Always a gift when there is a recurring theme. This means that we're on the track of internal voices and unconscious expression! Those sheets, what do they point to? This sounds more like Sleeping Beauty or a nighttime escape than like suicide . . . ?
35	Co	This conversation is going in the right direction for the kind of book I'm writing . . . But let's go back to what this means for *him*.
37	Co	I mean to say here that, in my view, he is concerned with questions such as "Am I doing it right?" and "What will other people think of me?", and at the same time I am thinking: what will he think of me?
	Cl	I feel listened to and understood.
38	Cl	His summary that this is an ethical issue and has something to do with integrity, sums up my introduction well.
39	Co	And now back to the personal!
42	Co	I will now try to summarise the essence of the last 25 minutes. And I am under an obligation to myself to speak fearlessly.
	Cl	His interventions: "reasons for thinking badly of you", "taking undue advantage" are intense. The word "badly" in particular continues to sound in my head. I think immediately: what is "badly"? and: whose "badly" is this, and: come on, surely it's not *that* bad? This seems to me more a personal than a professional reaction, which doesn't make it any less valuable to me. Here, a consultant is becoming visible in his system of values. That also makes him human.
43	Cl	I interpret the intervention "thinking badly", "taking advantage" mainly as a personal response of a colleague from the field. It immediately falls outside the context of this consulting relationship for me. That also says something, of course, about how I (do not!) allow myself to be led by him. It's as if a different part of Erik is coming to the fore, one that I don't know from my previous relationship with him. I notice that I am reflecting mainly about the consultant here. That can't be a good sign. This should in fact be an opportunity to reflect on myself.
47	Co	Phew – now I'm sounding very harsh in my own eagerness to speak fearlessly. Now it's becoming unpleasant for him – am I going too far? Every-

		thing I say about him here is also about me. Am I actually behaving with integrity?
	Cl	Interesting to note how an experienced consultant views my actions. If that's the way he sees things, perhaps many others will do too. That worries me.
49	Co	He doesn't look happy.
	Cl	I feel under attack by that comment: "may think badly of you".
50	Co	No, I don't agree with his comment that I am making it blacker than he is: what I have said is a summary of his own internal voice, which he himself has been very clear about. Just look at the dream.
	Cl	Is this the consultant now, or is it mainly Erik's personal opinion? Oh, is that what he actually thinks about it? Normally speaking, he responds with a lot more nuance; am I now seeing something of his real reaction?
51	Co	But that's not what I meant: I didn't want to talk about rules. I meant his own internal doubts, not rules outside himself. Can he accept that this is in fact a summary and not an opinion? All I am doing is summarising his black thoughts for him. For that matter, his thoughts are much blacker than in my summary: that people commit suicide because of his words, or that clients start to reject him as a person because of his interventions. He's thinking about his own relationship with "rules", and about "rules" in general, in order to think about something else, to distract himself from the disconcerting things that he has just heard.
52	Co	I'm facing resistance here, a lot of resistance, and very understandably. I have really let him have it, with my fearless speech. Fortunately he refers to the resistance himself, so he recognises it in himself.
54	Co	If resistance arises it is important to recontract.
55	Co	Now my feeling is that his resistance is turning into an attack: he calls me intense, while he has used this word intense four times already but always in relation to himself and his colleagues.
59	Co	He recognises something of that feedback of taking advantage – fortunately! He says "most true", he is honest and hard at work, so our connection seems strong enough. Let's see if I can use that strong connection for the next step: making the transference explicit.
	Cl	This isn't helping me yet to understand my internal process better: what can be a motive as a result of which my ethical decision-making process is sometimes disrupted? Is this about putting myself at the centre and wanting to raise my own profile at the expense of others, something I often struggled with even at secondary school?
62	Co	It's a relief that I can speak fearlessly about these doubts. I'm starting to worry about my relationship with Hendrik: will it be strong enough? In any case, this has become a real consulting conversation that affects both of us, so is entirely appropriate for the book.
65	Co	I seem to start stuttering when it's about me.
67	Co	I see this as a huge compliment from Hendrik. I have a huge feeling of relief when he says it was "great".

I think he also sees the risk to our relationship: "doesn't have to come to a stalemate".

70	Co	There he goes again. The resistance is still there as well.
73	Co	Hendrik is now summarising his emotions (in general terms).

He is now talking about the transference: making a connection between this conversation and his problem. Positive!

75	Co	I'm taking an enormous risk again here. I interrupt myself, but: too late. It has been said. I will now be causing unnecessary resistance.
76	Co	Hendrik is now starting to advise – he wants to become my consultant instead of the other way round.

But in a certain sense, talking about Bernadette, he now confirms my last hunch: it hasn't been "great" at all for him, here and now. This sort of thing is not great and he recognises that.

78	Co	I go back again to his doubts and struggles – and so almost miss something important that is happening in him here and now.
79	Co	He expresses himself very well again and at the same time gathers courage to say that the thing he wanted to say when I, careless as I was, interrupted him.

What am I doing here (mentioning the fact that I, also, was thinking of his sister)? Is this just for myself, to prove how "sensitive" I am? Or to show again that I was only summarising him and not interpreting? Why don't I let him touch upon the subject himself, at his own pace and in his own words – without immediately chipping in with the remark that I was thinking about it as well?

Or am I extending a bridge to him, by confirming that it is not silly for him to relate it to his sister?

I am inclined to call this my first ironic intervention in this conversation, because I show empathy for his association and softly chide him at the same time for being late with it.

End	Cl	The conclusion is about envy and competition: food for thought!

I am a bit disappointed that we are stopping here. That says something about the value of the conversation.

Observations following the conversation

1. The client's observations: based on Hendrik's notes
It is almost a month later. We haven't yet spoken to each other in detail and followed up the conversation. If it was really important, we could have done. I didn't consciously seek contact for a follow-up.

Is he only interested in getting a nice piece for his book, or does what we talked about really matter to him as well?

I do think it important to round that conversation off again. Preferably not in a consultant/client relationship, though. That is too unequal for me. I would like to know who I am really talking to. When Erik sug-gested that he may have reacted just as I did in the examples that I gave and that it reminded him of his relationship with his brother, he took the conversation out of the context of consulting to me. This is perhaps why you shouldn't confuse friendship and the consulting relationship. Although I am not normally one for strict role distinctions. Perhaps I'm afraid of losing Erik as a friend now: perhaps you're not entirely free to say whatever you think in the consulting relationship.

The question about my *Anliegen* and the question about the role that he could take as a consultant with respect to my issue, gave me trans-parency and helped me to reflect on what I expected of my consultant and the results of the conversation.

When I look back now at the word-for-word account of the conversa-tion, I think: what a lot of stuttering and stammering we did in the conversation. How insecure we both were about what we should say, and how. "Doing it right" seemed to be an important issue in the conversation.

My issue is really an existential one for me. I probably won't be able to solve it. I only hope that I'll be able to relate differently to it as the years pass: more aware of the traps I fall into and of my own contami-nating rationalisations.

2. The consultant's observations: based on Erik's notes

The shortest day in the year 2004 is a day that I won't forget in a hurry. The conversation was probing and rich. I am left with a sort of con-tentment after a completed assignment and the solemn feeling of having been in contact with a tragic theme. In the first hour after the conversation I am tense and preoccupied, preoccupied with whether it was too "intense", to use Hendrik's word. Preoccupied too with our relationship, whether it can stand such a far-reaching and personal consulting conversation. I say as much to Hendrik as we have a coffee together.

Then I notice how quickly I am able to put it out of my mind. The main impression that persists for the first few hours is that of a good conversation. I want to leave it to Hendrik to reap the benefits. Letting go (see Chapter 9) therefore turns out to be easy for me in this case.

What is also striking is that during the conversation I am already thinking about this book, and about how well or badly what happens in the conversation will turn out for the book. My feeling of contentment after the conversation is enhanced by the thought that it has been good for the book, which I think is a very selfish and not very client-oriented observation, comparable to the "inappropriate" and naughty thought of a possible follow-up assignment during other consulting conversations.

Then, when I begin looking back at the video, I realise that I actually used very few supporting interventions. It's true that I didn't flatter my client (compare Chapter 2), but I also failed to show any appreciation for his courage and honesty, for example, in:
- addressing underperforming colleagues;
- taking an honest and uncompromising look at himself;
- (later in the conversation) handling the challenging things I say to him.

In addition, I gave hardly any indication that I recognised his problems; I only did so for the first time after the transcribed section of the conversation. But I *am* happy with my fearless speech and the exploratory interventions that took place, and those appear to be at the right pace for Hendrik.

I also wonder what would have happened if I hadn't said some things at all, or had said them later, or rather much earlier, especially the fact that I was thinking about Hendrik's relationship with his sister (intervention 79).

While playing back and transcribing the video it also strikes me that I interrupt and direct my client more than I think. Despite the fact that I work with summaries and ask probing open questions, I appear to have interrupted his account a good six times. I find that I create a lot of resistance with my interventions. Then I used all sorts of tricks to suppress the resistance I caused:
- I refer back to our original contract (intervention 54).
- I defend myself by referring to the transference (intervention 59).
- I interpret the resistance and label it as positive (interventions 74 and 78).
- I bring myself up for discussion, stress my solidarity (interventions 61 and 79) and even mention my own relationship with my brother (after the transcribed section of the conversation).

Can this have to do with my countertransference (Chapter 10) in this situation? Perhaps Hendrik was behaving here in the same way he does with his clients and I let myself be seduced into giving the same response as his clients, or in any case the response that he says he fears in his clients, namely a critical, rejecting, interrupting response.

I also ask myself, while transcribing the text, how the subject-matter of the conversation relates to the book and what form of consulting has taken place here. In the first place, I notice that the entire conversation was about fearless speech (see Chapter 2) and the taking of intrinsic responsibility (see Chapter 8). I recognise those things as important themes of my own and more generally as themes that often preoccupy consultants. I also note that I opted for a coach role and an exploratory style of consulting as in the triangle model (see Chapter 6). I have the idea that this more personal approach fits in well with the very personal theme that Hendrik puts before me, but wonder at the same time what would have happened had I chosen a more distant and more progress-oriented approach, as would have been possible on the basis of the process management role.

The follow-up conversation

Our follow-up conversation consisted of two fairly long discussions that were probing once again. We talked about the differences between a consulting relationship and a friendship, about the possibility or otherwise of combining those two relationships, about competition, about the overstepping of personal boundaries, about showing one's feelings and about the consequences of this conversation for our friendship: we shared more emotions than we were accustomed to doing, we were able to keep listening to each other's emotions, and that ultimately brought us closer together.

Appendix A
Some Definitions of Consulting

Here are some definitions of consulting taken from current literature. Which definition best fits your consulting practice, and why? Circle the chosen definition. Or would you describe your work as a consultant differently? If so, add your own definition (7).

What is consulting?

(1) "Giving advice to someone who is faced with a choice."
(2) "Any form of providing help on a task where the consultant is not actually responsible for doing the task itself."
(3) "Using expertise to help clients narrow the gap between what they now have and what they want or need."
(4) "The art of influencing people at their request."
(5) "The creation of a relationship with the client that permits the client to perceive, understand, and act on events in order to improve the situation as defined by the client."
(6) "Licensed stupidity: asking naive questions."
(7) "..."

Sources of the six definitions of consulting

(1) is from Peter Block, in *Flawless consulting* (1981);
(2) is from Fritz Steele, in *Consulting for organizational change* (1975), and can also be found in Milos Kubr's *Management consulting – a guide to the profession* (1996);
(3) is from Geoffrey Bellman, in his book *The consultant's calling* (1990);
(4) is from Gerald Weinberg, in *The secrets of consulting* (1985);
(5) is from Edgar Schein, in *Process consultation* (1969);
(6) is from Anton Obholzer, in *The unconscious at work* (1994 – see the last page).

Looking from the perspective of the four consulting roles proposed in Chapter 5 of this book, we notice that:
- definition (1) is directed at the expert consultant;
- definitions (2) and (3) are more appropriate to the process manager;
- definition (4) best fits the developer; and
- definitions (5) and (6) give a good description of the coach's role.

Finally, here are a few more definitions of consulting to think over, borrowed from writers outside the consulting profession:
(7)   "Taking care that others take care of themselves" (Foucault, 1982).
(8)   "Just as there are people whose profession is to mourn for a fee, so also the gurus do things for the sake of others with detachment, without themselves being affected by them. The guru weeps with the weeping, laughs with the laughing, plays with the playful, sings with those who sing, keeping time to the song" (Sri Ramana Maharshi, 1985).

Both of these definitions fit in best with the role of coach, although they are also not out of place in the other roles.

Appendix B
Consulting Roles Questionnaire: Inventory of your Personal Role and Contribution as a Consultant

This questionnaire takes an inventory of:

- What you do as a consultant
- What you can do as a consultant
- What your main aim as a consultant is

It does not take an inventory of:

- What you want as a consultant
- What you see as your ideal consulting practice

In each case, divide 10 points over four different statements, based on your current practice. Don't spend too long considering your replies and base your answers on what you mainly do at present.

Example

1.a	I like to drink Italian wine with dinner.	2
1.b	I like to drink beer with my meals.	0
1.c	I prefer freshly squeezed orange juice with my dinner.	3
1.d	I tend to drink just water with meals.	5
	Total	10

List of statements

1.a   There are fields in which I regard myself an expert (e.g.
       logistics, IT, performance and benefits, recruitment).   *3*

1.b   My main expertise is developing people and
       people's competences, individually and/or in teams.   *2*

1.c   I am able to offer clients a "mirror" which
       generates new insights for them.   *1*

1.d   My main expertise lies in knowing how to manage
       projects or departments in such a way that they achieve
       the promised results.   *4*

2.a   I explore with others how best to approach a problem.   *3*

2.b   I help others to (re)define a problem by summarising
       their insights and feelings and exploring them further.   *2*

2.c   I help others by encouraging them to try out new things.   *1*

2.d   Others tend to delegate their problems to me: I then try
       to help them with my suggestions and knowledge.   *4*

3.a   In a consulting project, I feel really at home if I can
       ensure that others develop their skills and look for
       inspiration and new approaches.   *2*

3.b   In a consulting project, I feel really at home if I can
       monitor the progress of the work from a certain
       distance, occasionally providing suggestions regarding
       further improvement.   *3*

3.c   In a consulting project, I feel really at home if I can add
       value with new and much needed knowledge,
       information or solutions.   *3*

3.d   In a consulting project, I feel really at home if I can
       help individual members of the team or the team as a
       whole to be better integrated and aligned.   *2*

4.a   People that I work with are often unable to see their
       own shortcomings clearly, due to their own lengthy
       experience and accumulated expertise.   *3*

4.b   People that I work with are often very experienced and
       expert but insufficiently equipped in terms of their
       approaches and skills.   *2*

4.c   In my work I often deal with issues that are too
       complex as regards content for the people in the
       organisation.   *2*

4.d   I usually work in situations where people know what
       they want but not how to get there.   *3*

5.a   I report and then management takes a decision.   *2*

5.b   During decision-making I mostly discuss how that
       process itself can be improved: I reflect with others on
       the effects of their behaviours.   *3*

5.c   As a consultant I am mainly active after decision-
       making, when the time has come to actually undertake
       perilous actions.   *3*

5.d   I address shortcomings in the decision-making
       process and come up with proposals on how to
       improve it.   *2*

6.a   My job is often to encourage clients to take full
       responsibility for the things they wish to undertake.   *1*

6.b   My job is often to facilitate clients, individually or in
       teams, through times of significant change.   *3*

6.c   In my relationship with clients we often exchange
       detailed or complex information.   *2*

6.d   My job is often to build a strong personal relationship
       with my client in order that the client can accept
       personal feedback from me.   *4*

7.a	I help others to test or try out solutions which they have discovered.	2
7.b	My contribution is directed primarily at finding new problem-solving procedures, revealing shortcomings in the approaches taken and suggesting improvements.	3
7.c	My contribution is directed primarily at finding solutions to problems, so the quality of my advice depends on my knowledge of the issue at hand.	3
7.d	I help others to come to terms with solutions, for example, by helping them overcome resistance, anxiety or fear.	1
8.a	I usually let the client do the work; I hold up a mirror to reveal how that is going.	1
8.b	I usually let the client do the work; I support the client with advice and actions.	3
8.c	I usually let the client do the work; I create and offer new challenges.	2
8.d	My clients and I do most of the work together; I assume a guiding role but am, just as the client is, very active.	4
9.a	I enjoy my projects most if I see my input, whether ideas or solutions, being appreciated, adopted and implemented.	2
9.b	I enjoy my projects most if I see others being active, energised and motivated, without me having to give too much guidance or help.	4
9.c	I enjoy my projects most if I can help others to get on with the insights and opportunities they have developed themselves.	3
9.d	I enjoy my projects most if I see others gain new insights and discover new opportunities.	1

10.a   In my consulting practice I regularly facilitate meetings, away days or conferences.

2

10.b   In my consulting practice I regularly employ coaching, counselling and teambuilding methodologies.

3

10.c   In my consulting practice I regularly use research methodology, where I report back on the basis of diagnostic or survey data.

3

10.d   In my consulting work I regularly use training methodologies, didactical or "learning" approaches, or simulations.

2

11.a   I make others more aware of how their behaviour repeatedly leads them into the same problems – I help them to see the recurring patterns.

2

11.b   I bring others together in such a way that they can learn from each other.

2

11.c   I look for moments in which to communicate my knowledge and expertise.

3

11.d   I create opportunities and a context in which people can look at problems from another angle, e.g. by changing perspective, position, or role.

3

12.a   In projects I am often the one who knows best: I participate fully and frequently take the initiative.

1

12.b   In projects, rather than looking at the content, I often reflect with project leaders and teams on the way they work and the consequences thereof.

3

12.c   In projects, rather than looking at the content, my contribution generally focuses on phasing, the division of roles, project organisation, and monitoring progress.

3

12.d   In projects, rather than looking at the content, I often work with project leaders and teams on improving their ways of working.

3

13.a I help others to discover and develop alternative patterns of behaviour.   2

13.b My consulting focuses on complex strategic, organisational or managerial issues.   3

13.c Together with the client I look for promising directions for development.   3

13.d Together with the client I seek to uncover what is going on at a deeper level, usually a less visible level than that of knowledge, skills or behaviour.   2

14.a For me, an assignment is successful if lasting solutions have been found in a systematic and objective manner.   2

14.b For me, an assignment is successful if my clients have themselves become more able or skilful at solving their own problems.   3

14.c For me, an assignment is successful if my clients have obtained greater insight into their own problem-solving approaches.   2

14.d For me, an assignment is successful if my clients are satisfied with the quality of my advice.   2

15.a My approach to consulting draws primarily on my enthusiasm and didactic ability.   3

15.b My approach to consulting draws primarily on my expertise in specific areas.   2

15.c My approach to consulting draws primarily on my managerial experience and my ability to lead and inspire others.   2

15.d My approach to consulting draws primarily on my sensitivity and knowledge of people.   3

Score sheet

question	points	question	points	question	points	question	points
1.a	3	1.d	4	1.b	2	1.c	1
2.d	4	2.a	3	2.c	1	2.b	2
3.c	3	3.d	2	3.a	2	3.b	3
4.c	2	4.d	3	4.b	2	4.a	3
5.a	2	5.d	2	5.c	3	5.b	3
6.c	2	6.a	1	6.b	3	6.d	4
7.c	3	7.b	3	7.a	2	7.d	1
8.b	3	8.d	4	8.c	2	8.a	1
9.a	2	9.b	4	9.c	3	9.d	1
10.c	3	10.a	2	10.d	2	10.b	3
11.c	3	11.b	2	11.d	3	11.a	2
12.a	1	12.c	3	12.d	3	12.b	3
13.b	3	13.c	3	13.a	2	13.d	2
14.d	2	14.a	3	14.b	3	14.c	2
15.b	2	15.c	2	15.a	3	15.d	3
expert	38	process manager	41	developer	36	coach	34

(The total for the four columns should be 150 points.)

In a reliability study, I asked 68 consultants to complete this questionnaire. Approximately half of them were colleagues from Ashridge Consulting and the other half participants in the Ashridge open programme *Consulting for Change in Organisations*. The table below illustrates the distribution of the scores:

Consulting role	Minimum score:	Maximum score:	Average score:	Standard deviation:
Expert	4	67	31.0	15.1
Process manager	21	53	38.3	7.0
Developer	17	66	40.4	9.5
Coach	17	69	40.3	12.4

Most of the consultants in this population are (internal or external) organisation consultants. This may explain the higher scores for the last two roles, which focus more on the client and client organisation, but the bias may also come from the questions themselves. In any case, readers can now compare themselves with this control group (see also the graph below).

Detailed study of the replies from all 68 respondents shows that each individual item among the 60 items in total (4 per question, multiplied by 15 questions) leads to very different responses: with one exception, all items sometimes receive a "0" score (the one exception, 11.b, receives 1 point as its lowest score, and 8 as its highest score) and, again with just one exception, all items receive the highest score of the four options, i.e. 5 points or more (the exception in this case is 7.b, which receives a minimum of 0 and a maximum of 4 points). There were six items for which the score ranged from 0 to 10 points. This shows that all of the questions discriminate clearly for the consultant population tested.

Using the 68 completed forms, we were also able to test the questionnaire for internal consistency, by measuring Cronbach's Alpha. The results are given below:

Consulting role dimension	Cronbach's α:	Items that correlate negatively:	Cronbach's α without those items:
Expert	0.89	—	0.89
Process manager	0.37	3d, 4d, 6a	0.60
Developer	0.68	5c	0.73
Coach	0.83	3b	0.85

A Cronbach's Alpha higher than 0.7 is generally regarded as sufficiently consistent.[1] As the table shows, this questionnaire achieves such consistency for three of the four dimensions: only the questions about the process manager appear to measure different things. We are currently conducting measurements with a new, slightly amended questionnaire in the hope of achieving even better internal consistency. The first results of this preliminary study are encouraging: with 24 completed questionnaires we now have Cronbach's Alpha's of 0.89 (Expert), 0.65 (Process manager), 0.68 (Developer) and 0.87 (Coach).

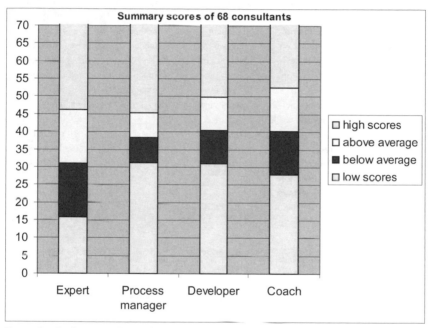

Scores for the four consulting roles of 68 consultants: the bands show the average scores plus and minus one standard deviation, so we expect approximately 70% of consultants to score within these bands for each dimension.

Finally, here is a summary of all of the different aspects, in terms of area of focus, client relationship, approach and methodology, which I associate with the four different consulting roles:

---

1   Due to the ipsative nature of the questionnaire, small deviations are possible. These deviations are negligible in my opinion because we correlate here only within a dimension and not between dimensions.

Roles: Aspects:	Expert	Process manager	Developer	Coach
Focused on	Content	Change	Improved skills	Enhanced insight
Relationship to client/ organisation	Consultant central	Collaborative	Strong and supportive	Client central
Division of labour with client or client organisation	• The consultant is active. • The client/ organisation provides information. • The consultant does the work and takes over responsibility. • The client/ organisation is sometimes dependent.	• The consultant, together with the client, makes roles explicit and carries out activities with a view to change. • The client/ organisation participates.	• The consultant challenges and gives feedback. • The client/ organisation experiments, practises.	• The consultant interprets and facilitates. • The client/ organisation discovers and takes action. • The consultant is sometimes detached and emphasises the responsibility of the client/ organisation.
Characteristics of consultant's approach	• research, analysis • comparing, benchmarking • putting forward solutions • contributing own knowledge and experience • adopting a central position	• structuring process • developing procedures • clarifying and assigning roles • suggesting approaches and methods • influencing preconditions for solution • drafting plans • discussing progress	• developing new patterns of behaviour • increasing scope for action • encouraging experimentation with new behaviour • developing skills • teaching interactively	• increasing problem-solving abilities • redefining problems • expanding frame of reference • developing insight into what is going on • exploring hidden assumptions

Roles: Aspects:	Expert	Process manager	Developer	Coach

Instruments/
interventions
	• research
	  methods
	• standards
	  and norms
	• key
	  performance
	  indicators
	• comparisons
	  with other
	  organisations/
	  sectors
	• writing
	  reports
	• presentations,
	  lectures
	• providing
	  literature
		• strategic
		  conferences
		• project
		  management
		• communication
		  techniques
		• harnessing
		  existing
		  knowledge
		• drafting
		  agendas
		• moderation
		  techniques
			• asking
			  questions,
			  listening
			• giving
			  supportive
			  feedback
			• confronting
			  and
			  challenging
			• offering
			  alternatives
			• training,
			  practising
			• teambuilding
			• survey-
			  feedback
			  methods
				• asking
				  questions,
				  listening
				• mirroring
				• interpreting
				• coaching,
				  counselling
				• pattern
				  analysis
				• psychometric
				  instruments
				• consultation
				  methods

References

1 Aeschylus (5th century BC). *Collected works*. Translations that I have perused: *Prometheus bound, The suppliants, Seven against Thebes, The Persians*, by P. Vellacott. The Penguin Classics, London, 1961. *The Oresteia – Agamemnon, The libation bearers, Eumenides*, by R. Fagles. The Penguin Classics, London, 1977.

2 Ahir, D.C. ed. (1999). *Vipassanā: a universal Buddhist meditation technique*. Indian Books Centre, Delhi.

3 Andrews, J.F. (1961). *Editor's introduction to King Lear*. In: *King Lear* (ed. J.F. Andrews). Doubleday Book & Music Clubs, Inc., New York.

4 Argyris, C. & Schön, D. (1978). *Organizational learning: a theory of action perspective*. Addison-Wesley, Reading (MA).

5 Aristophanes (405 BC): *Frogs*. In: *The complete plays of Aristophanes*. Bantam Classics, New York, 1962.

6 Aristotle (4th century BC). *The complete works of Aristotle – the revised Oxford translation* (ed. J. Barnes). Princeton University Press, Princeton (NJ), 1984.

7 Atkinson, J.B. & Sices, D. (ed. & transl., 1996). *Machiavelli and his friends. Their personal correspondence*. Northern Illinois University Press, DeKalb (IL).

8 Baddeley, S. & James, K. (1987). *Political skills for managers*. In: *Management Education and Development*, 18 pp. 3–19.

9 Baumgartel, H. (1959). *Using employee questionnaire results for improving organisations: the survey "feedback" experiment*. In: *Kansas Business Review*, 12 p. 6.

10 Bavelas, J.B., Black, A., Chovil, N. & Mullett, J. (1990). *Equivocal communication*. Sage, Newbury Park (CA).

11 Bell, C.R. & Nadler, L. eds (1979). *Clients and consultants*. Gulf Publishing, Houston.

12 Bellman, G.M. (1990). *The consultant's calling – bringing who you are to what you do*. Jossey-Bass, San Francisco.

13 Bentz, V.M. & Shapiro, J.J. (1998). *Mindful inquiry in social research*. Sage Publications, London.

14 Block, P. (1981). *Flawless consulting*. University Associates, San Diego.

15 Bradley, A.C. (1904). *Shakespearean tragedy – Lectures on Hamlet, Othello, King Lear, Macbeth*. Macmillan and Co., Limited, London.

16 Briggs Myers, I., McCaulley, M.H., Quenk, N.L. & Hammer, A.L. (1998). *MBTI manual*. CPP, Palo Alto (CA).

17 Carr, M., Curd, J. & Dent, F. (2005). *Ashridge MBTI research into distribution of type*. Ashridge Management College, Berkhamsted.

18 Corrigan, P. (1999). *Shakespeare on management – leadership lessons for today's managers*. Kogan Page Limited, London.

19 Craig, D. (2005). *Rip-off: the scandalous inside story of the management consulting money machine*. The Original Book Company, London.

20 Czander, W.M. (1993). *The psychodynamics of work and organizations*. Guilford Press, New York.

21 de Haan, E. (1999). Weldadig spreken met dubbele tong: ironie als techniek van de helpende buitenstaander bij veranderingen [Speaking benevolently with a "forked tongue": irony as a technique of the helping outsider in change]. In: *Filosofie in Bedrijf* 34, pp. 54–64.

22 de Haan, E. (2002). Machiavelli en de machtsspelen aan de top van de hiërarchie [Machiavelli and the power games at the top of the hierarchy]. In: *Filosofie* 12.5, pp. 2–16.

23 de Haan, E. (2004a). *The consulting process as drama – learning from King Lear*. Karnac Books, London.

24 de Haan, E. (2004b). *Learning with colleagues – an action guide to peer consultation*. Palgrave Macmillan, Basingstoke (UK).

25 de Haan, E. & Burger, Y. (2004). *Coaching with colleagues – an action guide to one-to-one learning*. Palgrave Macmillan, Basingstoke (UK).

26 DeVito, J.A. (1985). *Human communication – the basic course*. Harper & Row, New York.

27 Drucker, P.F. (1978). *Adventures of a bystander*. Heinemann, London.

28 Euripides (5th century BC). *Collected works*. Translations that I have perused: *Alcestis, Iphigenia in Tauris, Hippolytus*, by P. Vellacott. The Penguin Classics, London, 1953. *The Bacchae, Ion, The women of Troy, Helen*, by P. Vellacott. The Penguin Classics, London, 1954. *Medea, Hecuba, Electra, Heracles*, by P. Vellacott. The Penguin Classics, London, 1963. *The children of Heracles, Andromache, The suppliant women, The Phoenician women, Orestes, Iphigenia in Aulis*, by P. Vellacott. The Penguin Classics, London, 1972.

29 Foss, S.K., Foss, K.A. & Trapp, R. (1985). *Contemporary perspectives on rhetoric*. Waveland Press, Prospect Heights (IL).

30 Foucault, M. (1982). *Technologies of the self*, a lecture at the University of Vermont. Edited by L.H. Martin, H. Gutman & P.H. Hutton: *Technologies of the Self: A Seminar with Michel Foucault*. University of Massachusetts Press, Amherst (MA), 1988.

31 Foucault, M. (1983). *Parresia: free speech and truth*, six lectures delivered at the University of California at Berkeley. Edited by Joseph Pearson: *Fearless speech*. Semiotext(e), Los Angeles, 2001.

32 Foucault, M. (1984). *Le souci de soi*, part III of the *Histoire de la sexualité*. Gallimard, Paris. Translated as *The care of the self*, by R. Hurley. Penguin Books, London, 1986.

33 Freud, A. (1936). *Das Ich und die Abwehrmechanismen*. Vienna: Internationaler Psychoanalytischer Verlag. Translated as *The ego and the mechanisms of defence* by Cecil Baines. London: Hogarth Press.

34 Freud, S. (1912a). Zur Dynamik der Übertragung. Zentralblatt für Psychoanalyse, Vol. II. Translated as *The dynamics of transference* by James Strachey in collaboration with Anna Freud in *The standard edition of the complete psychological works of Sigmund Freud*, Volume XII, pp. 97–108.

35 Freud, S. (1912b). Ratschläge für den Arzt bei der Psychoanalytischen Behandlung. Zentralblatt für Psychoanalyse, Vol. II. Translated as *Recommendations to physicians practising psycho-analysis* by James Strachey in collaboration with Anna Freud in *The standard edition of the complete psychological works of Sigmund Freud*, Volume XII, pp. 109–120.

36 Freud, S. (1920). Zur Vorgeschichte der Analytischen Technik. In: Zeitschrift für Psychoanalyse, Band VI. Translated as *A note on the prehistory of the technique of analysis* by James Strachey in collaboration with Anna Freud in *The standard edition of the complete psychological works of Sigmund Freud*, Volume XVIII, pp. 263–265.

37 Hargie, O. ed. (1986). *A handbook of communication skills*. Croom Helm, Beckenham (UK).

38 Harrison, R. (1995). *Consultant's journey – a professional and personal odyssey.* McGraw-Hill, Maidenhead (UK).

39 Harrison, R. (1997). *A time for letting go.* In: *Organization Development Journal,* vol. 15.2, pp. 79–86.

40 Hutcheon, L. (1995). *Irony's edge: the theory and politics of irony.* Routledge, London and New York.

41 Isaacs, W. (1999). *Dialogue and the art of thinking together.* Random House, New York.

42 Isocrates (355 BC). *On the peace.* Translated by G. Norlin, § 113, in *Isocrates,* Vol. 2. Harvard and Heinemann, Cambridge (MA), 1968.

43 Karpman (1968). *Fairy tales and script drama analysis.* In: *Transactional analysis bulletin* 7.26, pp. 39–43.

44 Kierkegaard, S. (1841). *Om Begrebet Ironi med stadigt Hensyn til Socrates.* Edited and translated by H.V. Hong and E.H. Hong: *Concept of irony: with continual reference to Socrates.* Princeton University Press, Princeton (NJ), 1989.

45 Kolb, D.A. (1984). *Experiential learning – experience as the source of learning and development.* Prentice-Hall, Englewood Cliffs (NJ).

46 Kubr, M. ed. (1996). *Management consulting – a guide to the profession* (3rd revised edition). International Labour Office, Geneva.

47 Lawrence, W.G. (2000). *Tongued with fire – groups in experience.* Karnac Books, London.

48 Lear, J. (2003). *Therapeutic action – an earnest plea for irony.* Karnac Books, London.

49 Lewin, K. (1951). *Field theory in social sciences.* Harper & Row, New York.

50 Macdaid, G.P., McCaulley, M.H. & Kainz, R.I. (1986). *Atlas of type tables.* Center for Applications of Psychological Type, Gainesville (FL).

51 Machiavelli, N. (ca. 1514). *Il principe.* Translated by George Bull: *The prince.* The Penguin Classics, London, 1961.

52 Machiavelli, N. (ca. 1519). *Discorsi sopra la prima deca di Tito Livio.* Translated by Leslie Walker, then edited by Bernard Crick and revised by Brian Richardson: *The discourses.* The Penguin Classics, London, 1970.

53 Machiavelli, N. (1525). *Istorie Fiorentine* (1525). In: *Tutte le opere* (A cura di Mario Martelli). G.C. Sansoni, Firenze (1971).

54 Magerison, C.J. & Lewis, R.G. (1980). *Management educators and their clients.* In: *Advances in management education* (eds J. Beck & C. Cox), pp. 271–282. John Wiley & Sons, New York.

55 Malan, D.H. (1995). *Individual psychotherapy and the science of psychodynamics.* Butterworth-Heinemann, London.

56 Menzies, I.E.P. (1960). *A case-study in the functioning of social systems as a defence against anxiety: a report on a study of the nursing service of a general hospital.* In: *Human relations* 13, pp. 95–121.

57 Merton, R.K. & Barber, E.G. (2003). *The travels and adventures of serendipity: a study in sociological semantics and the sociology of science.* Princeton University Press, Princeton (NJ).

58 Miller, A. (1979). *Das Drama des begabten Kindes und die Suche nach dem wahren Selbst.* Suhrkamp, Frankfurt am Main. Translated as *The drama of being a child.* Virago, London, 1987.

59 Minuchin, S. (1974). *Families and family therapy.* Tavistock, London.

60 Najemy, J.M. (1993). *Between friends. Discourses of power and desire in the Machiavelli–Vettori letters of 1513–1515.* Princeton University Press, Princeton (NJ).

61 Nietzsche, F.W. (1872). *Die Geburt der Tragödie aus dem Geiste der Musik.* Band 1 van *Sämtliche Werke – Kritische Studienausgabe in 15 Bänden* (Herausg. d. G. Colli & M. Montinari). Deutscher Taschenbuch Verlag, München, 1980. Translated by

S. Whiteside as *Birth of tragedy: out of the spirit of music*. The Penguin Classics, London, 1993.

62 Nietzsche, F.W. (1885). *Also sprach Zarathustra*. Band 4 van *Sämtliche Werke – Kritische Studienausgabe in 15 Bänden* (Herausg. d. G. Colli & M. Montinari). Deutscher Taschenbuch Verlag, München, 1980. Translated by W. Kaufman as *Thus spoke Zarathustra: a book for all and none*. The Penguin Classics, London, 1976.

63 Nijk, A.J. (1978). *De mythe van de zelfontplooiing [The myth of self development]*. Boom, Meppel.

64 Nuttall, A.D. (1996). *Why does tragedy give pleasure?* Clarendon Press, Oxford.

65 Obholzer, A. & Zagier Roberts, V. (1994). *The unconscious at work*. Routledge, London.

66 O'Neill, M.B. (2000). *Coaching with backbone and heart*. Jossey-Bass, San Francisco.

67 Owen, H. (1997). *Open space technology*. Berret-Koehler, San Francisco.

68 Philodemos (around 50 BC). *Parrhesia / Fearless speech*. Translated as: *On frank criticism*, by D. Konstan, D. Clay, C.E. Glad, J.C. Thom and J. Ware. Scholars Press, Atlanta (Georgia), 1998.

69 Pinault, L. (2000). *Consulting demons*. HarperCollins, New York.

70 Plato (4th century BC). *Plato: complete works* (eds J.M. Cooper & D.S. Hutchinson). Hackett Publishing Company, New York, 1997.

71 Plutarch (109). *How to distinguish a flatterer from a friend*. Translated by R. Waterfield, in: *Essays*. The Penguin Classics, London, 1992.

72 Polti, G. (1895). *Les trente-six situations dramatiques*. Mercure de France, Paris. Translated by L. Ray as *The thirty-six dramatic situations*. Writer's Digest, Cincinnati (OH), 1931.

73 Quintilianus, M.F. (ca 94). *Institutio oratoria*. With English trans. by H.E. Butler. Loeb Classical Library, New York, 1921–1922.

74 Rogers, C.R. (1951). *Client-centered therapy: its current practice, implications, and theory*. Houghton Mifflin, Boston.

75 Rogers, C.R. (1961). *On becoming a person – a therapist's view of psychotherapy*. Constable, London.

76 Rosen, S. (1982). *My voice will go with you – the teaching tales of Milton H. Erickson, M.D.* W.W. Norton & Co., New York & London.

77 Rorty, R. (1989). *Contingency, irony and solidarity*. Cambridge University Press, Cambridge.

78 Schein, E.H. (1969). *Process consultation: its role in organization development*. Addison-Wesley, Reading (MA).

79 Schein, E.H., Schneier, I. & Barker, C.H. (1961). *Coercive persuasion*. W.W. Norton & Company, New York.

80 Schiller, F. (1803). *Über den Gebrauch des Chors in der Tragödie* – Preface to *Die Braut von Messina oder Die feindlichen Brüder*. Translation by A. Lodge in: *The bride of Messina: a tragedy with choruses*. John Bohn, London, 1841.

81 Schleiermacher, Fr.D.E. (1805–1833). *Hermeneutik [Hermeneutics]*. (Nach den Handschriften neu herausg. und eing. Von H. Kimmerle.) In: *Abhandlungen der Heidelberger Akademie der Wissenschaften – Philosophisch-historische Klasse II*, pp. 9–175 (1959).

82 Schön, D.A. (1983). *The reflective practitioner – how professionals think in action*. Basic Books, New York.

83 Schopenhauer, A. (1819). *Die Welt als Wille und Vorstellung*. Brockhaus, Leipzig. Translated by E.F.J. Payne as *The world as will and representation*. Falcon's Wing Press, Indian Hills (CO), 1958.

84 Schroder, M. (1974). *The shadow consultant*. In: *The Journal of Applied Behavioral Science*, 10.4, pp. 579–594.

85 Schulz von Thun, F. (1982). *Miteinander reden [Talking together]*. Reinbek bei Hamburg: Rowohlt.

86 Senzaki, N. & Reps, P. transcr. (1957). *Zen flesh, zen bones*. English edition: Shambhala, Boston & London.

87 Sophocles (5th century BC). *Collected works*. Translations that I have perused: *The three Theban plays* – Antigone, Oedipus the King, Oedipus at Colonus, by P. Fagles. The Penguin Classics, London, 1984. *Electra, Ajax, Women of Trachis, Philoctetes*, by E.F. Watling. The Penguin Classics, London, 1953.

88 Sri Ramana Maharshi (1985). *Be as you are* (ed. D. Godman). Arkana, London.

89 St. Augustine (398). *Confessions*. Translated by R.S. Pine-Coffin. The Penguin Classics, London, 1961.

90 Steele, F. (1975). *Consulting for organizational change*. University of Massachusetts Press, Amherst (MA).

91 Stroeken, H.P.J. (1988). *Kleine psychologie van het gesprek [Psychological compendium of the conversation]*. Boom, Amsterdam.

92 Thierry, H. (1965). *Organisatie en leiding [Organisation and leadership]*. Stenfert Kroese, Leiden.

93 Tilles, S. (1961). *Understanding the consultant's role*. In: Harvard Business Review, 39, pp. 87–99.

94 Thirlwall, C. (1833). *On the irony of Sophocles*. In: Philological Museum, 2, pp. 483–537.

95 Theophrastos (319 BC). *Characters*. Translated by P. Vellacott in *The characters by Theophrastus and plays and fragments by Menander*. The Penguin Classics, London, 1967.

96 Unamuno, M. de (1912). *Del sentimiento tragico de la vida*. Translated by J.E. Crawford Flitch in: *The tragic sense of life*. Dover publications, New York, 1921.

97 van Dongen, H.J., de Laat, W.A.M. & Maas, A.J.J.A. (1996). *Een kwestie van verschil [A matter of difference]*. Eburon, Delft.

98 Vellacott, P. (1975). *Ironic drama – a study of Euripides' method and meaning*. Cambridge University Press, London.

99 Visscher, K. & Rip, A. (1999). *Organisatie-adviseurs en de illusie van "agency" [Organisation consultants and the illusion of "agency"]*. In: M & O, January/February 1999, pp. 24–35.

100 von Schlegel, A.W. (1809). *Über dramatische Kunst und Literatur [On dramatic art and literature]*. Kritische Ausgabe (G.V. Amoretti). Kurt Schroeder Verlag, Bonn, 1923.

101 Walshe, M. (1987). *The long discourses of the buddha – a translation of the Digha Nikaya*. Wisdom Publications, Boston.

102 Watzlawick, P., Beavin, J. & Jackson, D.D. (1967). *Pragmatics of human communication*. W.W. Norton, New York.

103 Weinberg, G.M. (1985). *The secrets of consulting*. Dorset House Publishing, New York.

104 Zagier Roberts, V. (1994). *The self-assigned impossible task*. In: *The unconscious at work* (A. Obholzer & V. Zagier Roberts, eds). Routledge, London.

Index